Debbie Brown's
# Magical cakes

Debbie Brown's

# Magical cakes

MEREHURST

# Contents

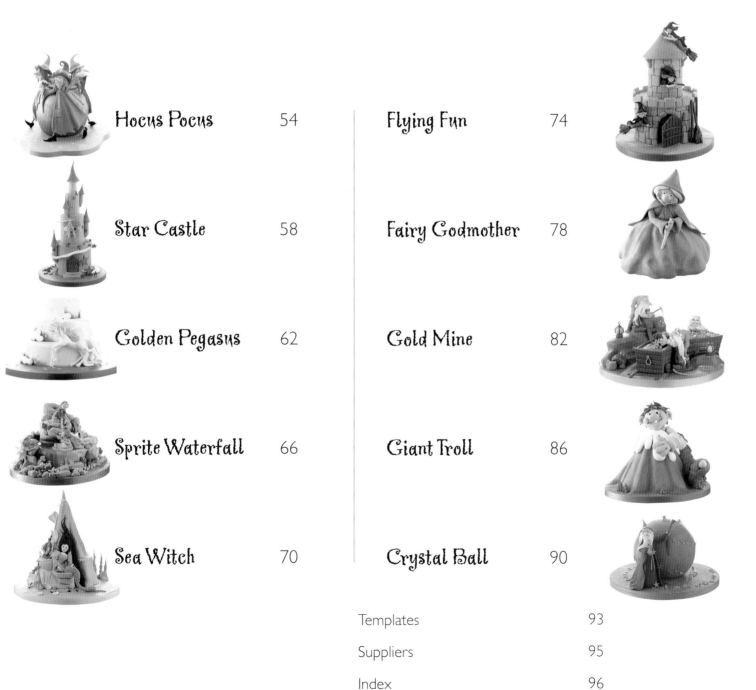

# Dedication

To Paul, with love

## Acknowledgements

Firstly, I would like to say thank you to my husband, Paul, for his unstinting support. The many hours sitting in traffic and transporting box after box containing fragile cakes to the centre of London, and getting them all there in one piece, is a feat in itself; and for his patience and understanding throughout the duration of producing the book, when the house is taken over by them.

Thank you to my best friends, Elaine and Aysa, and my mother Pam, who were all a little neglected during the intensity of producing this book, and warned not to call and chat for hours when the deadline loomed. We have a lot of catching up to do now!

As I can be very indecisive when it comes to anything creative, thank you to my daughter Laura for her impeccable taste in colour and design – she helped me clear my thoughts and go with first instincts. Thank you to my sons, Lewis and Shaun, for helping with all the research: they enlightened me on all the differences that there could be between these mythical creatures.

Many thanks to Barbara Croxford, a brilliant editor and very good friend, whose talent and professionalism shines through every time. Along with Barbara, thanks also to Catie Ziller and Shahid Mahmood, whose vision and creative minds helped form this beautiful book.

Thank you to Clive Streeter for the magical photographs and for his wit, charm and easygoing nature. He took the worry out of frantic days with hundreds of pieces needing to be arranged and photographed.

Thank you to Renshaw's for providing all the Regalice sugarpaste used throughout the book. A high quality sugarpaste that works as you want it to is invaluable. Thanks also to Edable Art, Squires Kitchen, Sugarflair and European Cake Gallery for their rainbow of wonderful edible powders, glitters and sparkles.

Last, but not least, a big thank you to all the people I have met through sugarcraft, especially my students, some of whom have become good friends. They keep me on my toes with anything new they would like to see and give me inspiration to keep producing books.

# Recipes & Materials

## Madeira sponge cake

The secret of successful cake decorating is to use a firm, moist cake that can be cut and shaped without crumbling. Madeira cake is a good choice and can be flavoured for variety. To make a madeira cake, follow the steps below. For the ingredients and bakeware required, see pages 12–13.

**1** Preheat the oven to 160°C/325°F/Gas 3, then grease and line the bakeware.

**2** Sift the self-raising and plain (all-purpose) flour together in a bowl. Put the softened butter and caster/superfine sugar in a large bowl and beat until the mixture is fluffy.

**3** Add the eggs to the mixture, one at a time with a spoonful of the flour, beating well after each addition. Add any flavourings required (see below).

**4** Using a large spoon, fold the remaining flour into the mixture. Spoon the mixture into the bakeware, then make a dip in the top of the mixture with the back of the spoon.

**5** Bake in the centre of the oven until a skewer inserted in the middle comes out clean (see pages 12–13 for baking times).

**6** Leave the cake to stand for about 5 minutes, then turn out onto a wire rack and leave to cool completely. When cold, store the cake in an airtight container until ready to use.

## Sugarpaste

I recommend using ready-made sugarpaste (rolled fondant), which is of high quality and is available from cake decorating suppliers (see page 95) and supermarkets. The sugarpaste used in this book is firm but pliable – it smoothes well and keeps its shape when drying. Try different sugarpastes to find your own preferences or use the recipe below.

To make 625g (1¼lb)
1 egg white, made up from dried egg albumen
30ml (2tbsp) liquid glucose
625g (1¼lb/4½cups) icing (powdered) sugar
A little white vegetable fat (shortening) if required

**1** Put the egg white and liquid glucose into a bowl, using a warm spoon for the liquid glucose.

**2** Sift the icing (powdered) sugar into the bowl, adding a little at a time and stirring continuously until the mixture thickens.

**3** Turn out the paste onto a work surface dusted with icing sugar and knead until it is smooth, soft and pliable. If the sugarpaste is dry and cracked, fold in a little vegetable fat (shortening) and knead again until it is smooth.

**4** Place in a polythene bag, or double wrap the paste in cling film (plastic wrap), and store in an airtight container until you are ready to use it.

### Madeira cake flavourings

- *Vanilla* Simply add 5ml (1tsp) of vanilla essence (extract) to every 6-egg mixture.
- *Lemon* Add the grated rind and/or the juice of 1 lemon to a 6-egg mixture.
- *Almond* Add 5ml (1tsp) of almond essence and 30–45ml (2–3tbsp) of ground almonds to a 6-egg mixture.
- *Chocolate* Add 30–45ml (2–3tbsp) of unsweetened cocoa powder mixed in 15ml (1tbsp) of milk to a 6-egg mixture.
- *Chocolate swirl* Fold 155g (5oz) of dark melted cooking chocolate, or 75g (2½oz) each of melted white and dark cooking chocolate, into a 6-egg mixture until marbled.
- *Golden syrup* Replace each 60g (2oz) of caster sugar with 25ml (1 heaped tbsp) of golden syrup.

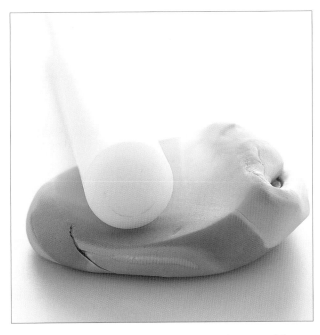

*Marbling together different colours of sugarpaste (see page 54).*

## Buttercream

As well as making a delicious filling between layers of cake, a thin coat of buttercream, spread all over the cake, fills any small gaps and also provides a smooth surface on which to apply the sugarpaste. Buttercream can also be flavoured (see below).

To make about 500g (1lb/2 cups)
125g (4oz/½ cup) butter, softened
15ml (1tbsp) milk
375g (12oz/2¾ cups) icing (powdered) sugar

**1** Put the softened butter into a mixing bowl. Add the milk and/or any flavouring required (see Buttercream flavourings, below).

**2** Sift the icing (powdered) sugar into the bowl, a little at a time, and beat well after each addition, until all the sugar has been incorporated and the buttercream has a light, creamy texture.

**3** Store the buttercream in an airtight container until it is required.

## Modelling paste

Modelling paste is made by incorporating an edible gum into sugarpaste. The gum is available in powder form and is easily kneaded into the sugarpaste, which makes the paste much firmer but still pliable. You can model items using just sugarpaste, but modelling paste keeps its shape well and dries much harder, giving strength to your finished work.

The natural gum, gum tragacanth, or the manmade alternative, CMC (carboxy methyl cellulose), were employed to make the modelling paste that is used in this book. Both are widely used in the food industry as thickeners. Gum tragacanth needs a little time after it has been kneaded into sugarpaste before the gum starts to work, usually around 4–8 hours. CMC, on the other hand, starts to work virtually straight away and is slightly stronger and cheaper. There are also some ready-made modelling pastes available that give good results. All these items are available from cake decorating suppliers.

To make 500g (1lb) modelling paste
10ml (2tsp) gum tragacanth or 5–7ml (1–1½tsp) CMC
500g (1lb) sugarpaste (rolled fondant)

**1** Sprinkle the powder onto a work surface and knead into the sugarpaste (rolled fondant).

**2** Double wrap the modelling paste in cling film (plastic wrap) or polythene and keep airtight until it is required.

## Royal icing

Royal icing is used to pipe fine details, as well as hair and sea foam, and for sticking items firmly together. Ready-made royal icing can be obtained in powder form (follow the instructions on the packet). You may prefer to make your own, following the royal icing recipe below.

To make about 280g (9oz)
1 egg white, made up from dried egg albumen
250–280g (8–9oz/2 cups) icing (powdered) sugar

**1** Put the egg white into a bowl. Beat in the icing (powdered) sugar, a little at a time, until the icing is firm and glossy, and forms peaks when the spoon is pulled out.

**2** Place a damp cloth over the top of the bowl for a few minutes or until you are ready to use it – this will prevent the icing from crusting.

*Royal icing piped in waves for hair.*

---

### Buttercream flavourings

- *Vanilla*  Add 5ml (1tsp) of vanilla essence (extract).
- *Lemon*  Replace the milk with 15ml (1tbsp) of fresh lemon juice.
- *Chocolate*  Mix the milk and 30ml (2tbsp) of unsweetened cocoa powder to a paste and add to the mixture.
- *Coffee*  Mix the milk and 15ml (1tbsp) of instant coffee powder to a paste and add to the buttercream mixture.

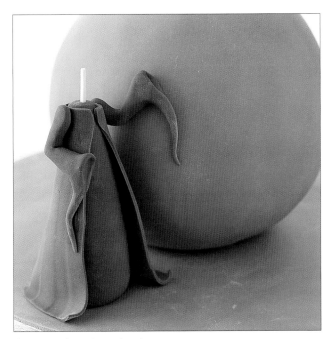

*A sugar stick used as a head support.*

## Sugar sticks

Support is sometimes required when building up modelled items. Sugar sticks can be used to help hold such pieces in place. They are quick and easy to make, although some drying time is required. Alternatively, raw, dried spaghetti can be used.

To make 10–20 sugar sticks
1.25ml (¼tsp) CMC or gum tragacanth
5ml (1tsp) royal icing

Knead the CMC or gum tragacanth into the royal icing until the mixture thickens and forms a paste. Roll it out and cut into different-sized strips of various lengths, using a clean straight-bladed knife. To prevent untidy edges and crumbling occurring, roll the knife down through the paste. Alternatively, roll the paste into thin sausage shapes. Leave to dry for 4–8 hours before use.

## Sugar glue

Sugar glue is required to stick pieces of sugarpaste together. Egg white made up from powdered egg albumen is a good glue, as is royal icing or sugarpaste and water mixed together.

Alternatively, a glue made from CMC is popular, which is available from cake decorating suppliers. Mix 1.25ml (¼tsp) CMC powder with 15–30ml (1–2tbsp) of water to make a transparent gel. Keep in an airtight container in the refrigerator and use within one week.

To stick sugarpaste pieces together, slightly dampen the paste with sugar glue using a fine paintbrush. Gently press them into position, holding for a few moments. Small pieces of foam sponge can be used to support the pieces while they are drying.

## Food colouring paste

I recommend the use of food colourings in concentrated paste form, as they do not change the consistency of the sugarpaste. These food colourings can be obtained in a rainbow of colours from cake decorating suppliers and many supermarkets.

## Powder food colouring

I only use powder food colouring as a subtle addition to the already coloured sugarpaste, and apply when the cake is completely dry. With the exception of metallic colours, mix the powder food colouring with a little icing sugar to prevent blotching. Brush over the surface of the cake, a little at a time, with either a dusting brush or a medium-sized sable paintbrush, until the required vibrancy is achieved.

With metallic powders, you can concentrate colouring and give a bright sheen by rubbing over the surface with your fingers. When a really bright area is required, paint a little sugar glue over the surface and leave until tacky, then brush on the powder with a medium-sized sable paintbrush. Edible metallic paint is also available.

Sparkle powder is a very fine edible powder, which spreads easily over the surface of the cake, making it shimmer and sparkle. This powder is also obtainable added to powdered colours.

## Edible glitter

I have used edible glitters and sparkles throughout this book, which give a wonderful vibrant sparkle to the finished cake, especially in sunlight or when placed directly under artificial light. Although these glitters are edible, I have kept their addition subtle as a little goes a long way and, in most projects, just concentrated the glitter over the cake board instead of the cake.

Make sure you purchase edible glitters from specialist cake decorating outlets and that they state they are edible on the pot, or clarify when purchasing. With food safety standards often changing, I would not recommend the use of products that have been previously bought and then kept for any length of time.

### Storing the decorated cake

Mix equal parts (¼-½ tsp) gum arabic, water and edible metallic or coloured sparkle powder. Brush mix onto a nonstick ovenproof liner and bake on a low heat until dry and peeling. Lift with a palette knife and push through a sieve to make glitter.

# Basic Equipment & Techniques

**Ball or bone tool** is used to indent circles into paste. When the bone tool handle is down, it will indent a teardrop.

**Cake smoother** is used to create a smooth surface on sugarpaste (rolled fondant). The type with a handle is the most useful. Smooth it over the paste in a circular motion to level out an uneven surface.

**Circle cutter** is used to cut out or indent various circular shapes. Pressed in at an angle, it will indent semi-circles for smiles.

**Cocktail sticks** (toothpicks) are ideal for indenting small details and also handy for applying food colouring to sugarpaste.

**Daisy cutter** is used for fairy costumes and crowns.

**Dusting brush** is used to apply a concentrated amount of powder food colouring.

**Foam sheet** is useful for drying modelled items or figures because the air can circulate underneath and dry them more quickly.

**Foam sponge** is for supporting decorative pieces while they are drying (see photograph).

**Food-safe plastic dowelling** can be used to internally support cakes that are built up.

**Kitchen paper** protects the cake from excess powder colouring when brushed over a specific area.

**Paintbrushes** are essential for painting and dusting the cakes, and marking details using the handle. Use good quality sable paintbrushes for best results, especially when painting fine details. Paintbrushes have numbered sizes: Nos 00–1 (fine), Nos 2–4 (medium) and Nos 5–6 (large).

**Piping bags** use parchment or greaseproof paper piping bags in preference to plastic.

**Piping tubes** have been used throughout the book not only to pipe fine details, but also as miniature circle cutters and to indent semi-circles when pressed into paste at an upward angle.

**Plain-bladed knife** is essential for making clean, accurate cuts in cakes and various pastes.

**Rolling pins** (large and small) are essential for rolling out paste. White polypropylene pins are recommended.

**Ruler** is used for accurately measuring and cutting sugarpaste shapes. Also used for indenting neat lines.

**Scissors** are needed for cutting out templates and some modelling.

**Serrated knife** is used for carving and cutting the cake.

**Small glue brush** for applying sugar glue. Smaller sizes can get into awkward areas. (I use my older good quality paintbrushes, sizes 1–3.)

**Small scourer** is used to indent texture on the surface of paste.

**Square cutter** is used to cut out square shapes, such as windows, doors and bricks.

**Star cutter** is used to make star shapes, flowers and sprite wings.

**Sugar shaker** filled with icing (powdered) sugar is used for sprinkling controlled amounts when required, especially when rolling out sugarpaste.

*A piece of foam sponge is used as a support until dry.*

## CUTTING & SHAPING CAKES
### Cake sculpting
To sculpt cake into different shapes, use a serrated knife. Cut a little at a time, shaving off small pieces unless otherwise directed, until you have the required shape. If you shave off more than you need, pieces of cake can be stuck back on with a little buttercream, but take care not to do this too much as it may cause the sugarpaste (rolled fondant) to slip when applied.

*To cut accurate shapes, use a serrated knife.*

### Balance
When building up a high cake, make sure each layer is completely straight and that the cake is perfectly balanced. If part of the cake is left only slightly uneven, it will look much worse when covered with sugarpaste and may cause the cake to lean.

## USING SUGARPASTE
### Colouring the paste
Add food colouring to the sugarpaste a little at a time with a cocktail stick (toothpick). Knead it into the sugarpaste, adding more until you have the required shade. Wear plastic gloves as the food colouring can temporarily stain your hands. Pre-coloured packs of sugarpaste are now obtainable from cake decorating suppliers and many supermarkets.

### Preparing and handling sugarpaste
Knead thoroughly until warm and pliable before rolling out onto a work surface covered with a sprinkling of icing (powdered) sugar. Keep moving the paste around so that it does not stick and roll it to a thickness of 3–4mm (⅛–⅙in), unless otherwise stated.

To lift a large piece of rolled-out sugarpaste, lay a large rolling pin on the centre and flip the paste over it. Lift it, position, then roll the paste into place. Use a sharp, plain-bladed knife to cut the paste. To avoid the paste 'pulling', cut cleanly downwards. Keep wiping the blade to remove excess, or a layer of paste will build up and make the cuts untidy.

### Covering the cake board
Roll out the sugarpaste, lift and cover the board. Use a cake smoother to give a smooth surface. If the paste has not stuck to the board, lift the sugarpaste around the edge and moisten with a damp paintbrush. Trim any excess downwards with a sharp knife.

You may wish to remove the sugarpaste from the area of the board on which the cake will sit. Because the cake is moist, the sugarpaste beneath has a tendency to become sticky. Leave coated cake boards to dry for at least 12 hours.

### Covering the cake
Spread a layer of buttercream over the surface of the cake to help the sugarpaste stick. Roll out sugarpaste and cover the cake completely, smoothing around the shape and trimming any excess. Pleats can be stretched out but I recommend cutting stubborn pleats away when covering awkward shapes. This will leave a join, so press together until only a thin line remains, then rub gently with a little icing sugar on your fingertips until completely removed. If required, rub the surface with a cake smoother to produce a smooth surface.

When dry, polish the surface with your hands to remove excess icing sugar and give a sheen. Stubborn marks can be removed with a damp paintbrush.

*For easy positioning, lift sugarpaste with a rolling pin.*

| CAKE | PAGE | BAKEWARE | EGGS | SELF-RAISING FLOUR | PLAIN/ALL-PURPOSE FLOUR | BUTTER, SOFTENED | CASTER/SUPERFINE SUGAR | BAKING TIME |
|---|---|---|---|---|---|---|---|---|
| Emerald City | 22 | 3 x 15cm (6in) round tins | 6 | 375g (12oz/ 3 cups) | 185g (6oz/ 1½ cups) | 375g (12oz/ 1½ cups) | 375g (12oz/ 1½ cups) | I hour |
| Pirate Dreams | 42 | 20cm (8in) square tin | 4 | 250g (8oz/ 2 cups) | 125g (4oz/ I cup) | 250g (8oz/ I cup) | 250g (8oz/ I cup) | I hour |
| Gold Mine | 82 | 20cm (8in) square tin | 5 | 315g (10oz/ 2½ cups) | 155g (5oz/ 1¼ cups) | 315g (10oz/ 1¼ cups) | 315g (10oz/ 1¼ cups) | 1¼–1½ hours |
| Hocus Pocus | 54 | 2 x I litre (2 pint/ 5 cup) ovenproof bowls | 5 | 315g (10oz/ 2½ cups) | 155g (5oz/ 1¼ cups) | 315g (10oz/ 1¼ cups) | 315g (10oz/ 1¼ cups) | 1¼ hours |
| Crystal Ball | 90 | | | | | | | |
| Flying Fun | 74 | 2 x 15cm (6in) round tins 18cm (7in) round tin (evenly fill each tin) | 6 | 375g (12oz/ 3 cups) | 185g (6oz/ 1½ cups) | 375g (12oz/ 1½ cups) | 375g (12oz/ 1½ cups) | I hour each |
| Wizard's Helpers | 46 | 10cm (4in) round tin 15cm (6in) round tin 20cm (8in) square tin (put half of mixture in 20cm (8in) tin, then fill remaining tins) | 7 | 440g (14oz/ 3½ cups) | 220g (7oz/ 1¾ cups) | 440g (14oz/ 1¾ cups) | 440g (14oz/ 1¾ cups) | 50 mins– I hour largest tin 1–1¼ hours other tins |
| Baby Dragon | 51 | 3 x 625ml (1¼ pint/ 3 cup) ovenproof bowls (fill two bowls evenly and third bowl with 60ml (4tbsp) of mixture) | 4 | 250g (8oz/ 2 cups) | 125g (4oz/ I cup) | 250g (8oz/ I cup) | 250g (8oz/ I cup) | I hour each 30 mins smaller bowl |

| CAKE | PAGE | BAKEWARE | EGGS | SELF-RAISING FLOUR | PLAIN/ALL-PURPOSE FLOUR | BUTTER, SOFTENED | CASTER/ SUPERFINE SUGAR | BAKING TIME |
|---|---|---|---|---|---|---|---|---|
| Sea Witch | 70 | 10cm (4in) round tin 12cm (5in) round tin 18cm (7in) round tin (evenly fill each tin) | 6 | 375g (12oz/ 3 cups) | 185g (6oz/ 1½ cups) | 375g (12oz/ 1½ cups) | 375g (12oz/ 1½ cups) | 1–1¼ hours each |
| Golden Pegasus | 62 | 10cm (4in) round tin 15cm (6in) round tin 20cm (8in) round tin (evenly fill each tin) | 6 | 375g (12oz/ 3 cups) | 185g (6oz/ 1½ cups) | 375g (12oz/ 1½ cups) | 375g (12oz/ 1½ cups) | 1 hour each |
| Rock Monster | 18 | | | | | | | 40 mins smallest tin |
| Ramshackle Village | 26 | 25cm (10in) square tin | 7 | 440g (14oz/ 3½ cups) | 220g (7oz/ 1¾ cups) | 440g (14oz/ 1¾ cups) | 440g (14oz/ 1¾ cups) | 1¼ hours |
| Star Castle | 58 | | | | | | | |
| Wizard Owl | 34 | 25cm (10in) square tin | 6 | 375g (12oz/ 3 cups) | 185g (6oz/ 1½ cups) | 375g (12oz/ 1½ cups) | 375g (12oz/ 1½ cups) | 1 hour |
| Labyrinth | 38 | | | | | | | |
| Sprite Waterfall | 66 | 10cm (4in) round tin 20cm (8in) round tin (evenly fill each tin) | 4 | 250g (8oz/ 2 cups) | 125g (4oz/ 1 cup) | 250g (8oz/ 1 cup) | 250g (8oz/ 1 cup) | 1 hour larger tin |
| King Neptune | 30 | | | | | | | 40 mins smaller tin |
| Giant Troll | 86 | 18cm (7in) round tin 20cm (8in) round tin (evenly fill each tin) | 6 | 375g (12oz/ 3 cups) | 185g (6oz/ 1½ cups) | 375g (12oz/ 1½ cups) | 375g (12oz/ 1½ cups) | 1 hour larger tin |
| Dragon Castle | 14 | | | | | | | 50 mins smaller tin |
| Fairy Godmother | 78 | 2 litre (4 pint/ 10 cup) ovenproof bowl | 5 | 315g (10oz/ 2½ cups) | 155g (5oz/ 1¼ cups) | 315g (10oz/ 1¼ cups) | 315g (10oz/ 1¼ cups) | 1¼–1½ hours |

Refer to page 7 for madeira cake instructions.
All baking tins used are 8cm (3in) depth.
All ovenproof bowls used are Pyrex.

# Dragon Castle

Dragons are always rather frightening in mythology, so I designed this one to appeal to someone older. Although I'm sure that smaller children would love the thrill of this scary beast.

## Cake & decoration

(See pages 7–13 for recipes and cake chart)

18cm (7in) and 20cm (8in) round cakes

25cm (10in) round cake board

440g (14oz/1¾ cups) buttercream

1.25kg (2½lb) sugarpaste (rolled fondant)

Cream, black, orange, green and brown food colouring pastes

Icing (powdered) sugar in a shaker

Sugar glue

625g (1¼lb) modelling paste

Red and green powder food colourings

Edible gold powder

## Equipment

Plain and serrated kitchen knives

4cm (1½in) and 5cm (2in) circle cutters

Large rolling pin

Small glue brush

1cm (½in) square cutter

Templates (see page 94)

A few cocktail sticks

Pieces of foam sponge

Medium paintbrush

New small flexible scourer

Dusting brush

## Castle

**1** Trim the crust from both cakes, level the tops and cut a layer in each. Cut the smaller cake in half and place one half on top of the larger cake. Trim around the cake, creating sloping sides, and place on the cake board. From the remaining half, cut three circles, two using the 4cm (1½in) cutter and the third with the 5cm (2in) cutter, and sandwich the two smaller circles together with buttercream to make the tall tower. Sandwich all layers together (see a) and spread a thin layer of buttercream over the surface of all cakes to help the sugarpaste (rolled fondant) stick.

**2** Colour 1kg (2lb) of sugarpaste dark cream, kneading until the colour is marbled and nearly blended. Put the two tower cakes aside. Roll out and cover the cake and cake board completely, smoothing around the shape, then trim excess from around the

a

edge. For a rock effect, slice a very thin piece of sugarpaste from the surface of the covering in small amounts around the cake sides, taking care not to cut too deep and reveal the cake underneath (see b). Indent at the front to make a recess for the winding steps.

## Towers and doors

**3** Colour 250g (8oz) of sugarpaste pale cream. Roll out 220g (7oz) and cut strips to cover around the sides of both towers, smoothing the joins closed. To remove the joins completely, rub gently in a circular motion with a little icing sugar on your fingertips. To cover the tops, roll out 30g (1oz), place the top of each tower down onto it and cut around. Stick each tower onto the cake using a little sugar glue.

**4** Cut out a doorway in each tower using the templates. Colour 7g (¼oz) of modelling paste black, thinly roll out and cut pieces to fill both. Reserve the

trimmings for later. Colour 265g (8½oz) of modelling paste pale cream. Roll out 45g (1½oz) and cut strips to fit around the top of each tower, 2cm (¾in) in depth. From the top of each, cut out small squares with the 1cm (½in) square cutter. Mark slits for windows using the tip of a knife, then stick around the top of each tower, smoothing the join closed. Mark longer windows on the towers.

**5** With 125g (4oz) of pale cream modelling paste, and using the step photograph as a guide (see c), make four different-sized towers, marking slit windows on each as before. Indent little doorways and fill with black modelling paste trimmings. Colour 75g (2½oz) of modelling paste deep cream. Make four different-sized pointed roofs using 60g (2oz), then stick onto the top of each tower.

**6** With pale cream trimmings, roll two sausages to edge the top of each doorway, rolling each

thinner in the centre and bend halfway. Thickly roll out 60g (2oz) of pale cream modelling paste and cut the stepped archway using the template (see page 94). For the steps winding down the front of the cake, cut little strips graduating in size using 7g (¼oz) of pale cream, and stick in place. With the remaining pale cream, make the doorstep and cut strips for the arches, bend round and re-cut the ends so they sit against the cake sides. With trimmings, model some oval-shaped stones for around the base of the castle. Make some more, using the deeper cream, and cut little strips for windowsills.

## Dragon

**7** Colour 250g (8oz) of modelling paste orange. For the dragon's body, roll 100g (3½oz) into a tapering sausage, 35cm (14in) in length. Immediately stick in place, winding around the castle with the neck end resting on top of the small tower and leaving room for the head. Shape the dragon's head

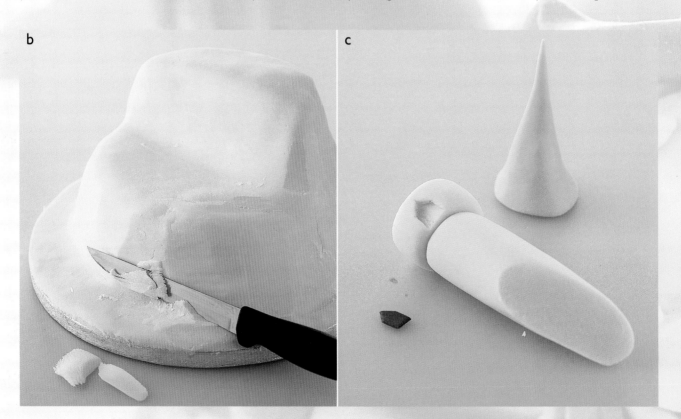

using 22g (¾oz) of orange modelling paste, cutting his mouth open with a knife. Wedge a small piece of foam into the mouth until set. Using the step photograph as a modelling guide (see d), model all the facial features. Remove the piece of foam before applying the teeth and rub gently at each join to remove. To make the fans either side and at the back of his head, indent into flattened teardrop shapes using the paintbrush handle, then pinch up little points in between. Colour 15g (½oz) of modelling paste green. Using a tiny amount with a little black modelling paste, make his eyes.

8 Split 7g (¼oz) of orange modelling paste into three pieces. Shape the triangular point for the end of his tail with one piece, indenting twice with the paintbrush handle. Make the arms with the other two pieces. First, roll into sausages, rounding off one end. Cut twice into the top and pinch out three claws. For feet,

split another 7g (¼oz) in half and roll into sausage shapes. Bend each half way and press one half flat, pinching out a heel at the back. Cut twice at the end of each foot and pinch out three claws. Using 7g (¼oz) of orange, shape different-sized, flattened oval shapes for scales and stick over the dragon's back, with the larger scales down the centre.

## Dragon's wings and trees

9 Split the remaining orange modelling paste in half and use for the two wings. To make the wings, use the template and step photograph (see e). Use the handle of the paintbrush, rolled over the surface, to indent the ridges. Stick each wing in place, holding for a few moments until secure, or use small pieces of foam sponge to support until dry. Colour the remaining modelling paste brown and, with the remaining green, make six trees in different sizes, texturing the green by rolling over the scourer.

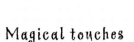

## Magical touches

10 Mix red and green powder colours separately with a little icing sugar. Dust red over the dragon, keeping the colour more concentrated centrally down his back. Dust a little green powder colour onto the cake board, around the base of the trees. Randomly dust the whole cake and dragon with gold powder.

d

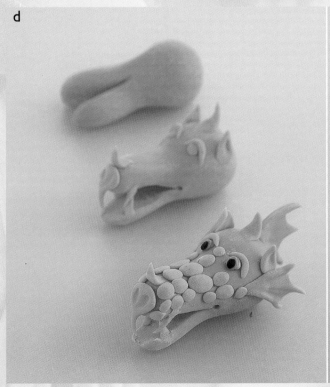

e

# Rock Monster

I nearly put this trio of elfins camping down for the night beside a friendly rock monster. But I thought I would make it a little scary, so they all became dinner instead!

## Cake & decoration

(See pages 7–13 for recipes and cake chart)

10cm (4in), 15cm (6in) and 20cm (8in) round cakes

35cm (14in) round cake board

1.75kg (3½lb) sugarpaste (rolled fondant)

Blue, black, brown, cream, green and egg yellow food colouring pastes

Icing (powdered) sugar in a shaker

470g (15oz/scant 2 cups) buttercream

Sugar glue

140g (4½oz) modelling paste

Dark green and egg yellow powder food colourings

Edible sparkle powder

## Equipment

Large rolling pin

Plain and serrated kitchen knives

Small glue brush

A few cocktail sticks

Fine paintbrush

Pieces of foam sponge

Dusting brush

### Cake board and cake

1 Colour the sugarpaste (rolled fondant) blue/grey using a touch each of blue and black food colouring pastes. Roll out 500g (1lb) and cover the cake board completely, marking an uneven surface by pressing with the rolling pin, then trim excess from around the edge. Trim the crust from each cake and level the tops. Cut the top edge from the two larger cakes and stack one on top of the other. Trim the small cake to round the top, then cut into the sides to create an uneven surface. Position on top of the other cakes, slightly towards the back.

### Rock monster

2 To shape the mouth, remove a wedge from the top of the second cake and trim a curved line at the front to round off a full bottom lip (see a). Place the cake on the board, slightly towards the back. Use

a

cake trimmings to fill out around the base of the cake. Sandwich the layers together with buttercream, then spread a layer over the surface of the cakes to help the sugarpaste stick. For the rock feet, make two piles of cake trimmings and spread completely with buttercream, filling any gaps.

**3** Roll out 875g (1¾lb) of blue/grey sugarpaste and cover the cake completely, smoothing the paste into the mouth recess and around the shape. Trim excess from around the base and press the knife around the edge to curve it under. Roll out 90g (3oz) and cover the two remaining feet cakes, trim excess around the base and then position on the cake board.

**4** For the rock hands, split 125g (4oz) of blue/grey sugarpaste in half and shape into rounded teardrop shapes. Curve each round slightly and stick against the sides of the rock, near the corners of the mouth. Split 30g (1oz) and model angular rocks for arms. Using 100g (3½oz), model different-sized angular rocks and stick in position around the cake, piling a few on top of his head. Using the step photograph as a guide *(see b)* and the blue/grey trimmings, model all the shapes to build up his facial features, colouring his pupils a slightly darker shade of grey.

**5** Colour 7g (¼oz) of modelling paste dark brown. Roll different-sized twigs for the fire and three twigs for the backpacks, marking the surface of each with a knife. Arrange the fire twigs in a circle at the front of the cake board. Put aside the twigs for the backpacks to allow to dry.

## Elfins

**6** To make the elfins, first colour 45g (1½oz) of modelling paste cream. For bodies, split just under 7g (¼oz) in half and model two oval shapes. Stick one on top of each rock hand, filling the recess. Colour pea-sized amounts of modelling paste green. Roll out into triangle shapes and indent pleats with a cocktail stick (toothpick) for tunics, sticking the point of the triangle over one shoulder.

**7** To make the heads, using the step photograph as a guide *(see c)*, roll 7g (¼oz) for each into oval shapes and then pinch out long noses. Push the end of a paintbrush into each mouth area and move up and down to open them wide. Colour a minute piece of modelling paste black and shape four tiny oval-shaped eyes. Edge the top and bottom of each eye with tiny tapering sausage shapes. For ears, model teardrop shapes using pea-sized amounts, and indent in the centre of each. Pinch the ears at the pointed end to lengthen, then stick in place level with the nose.

b

c

**8** Colour just over 7g (¼oz) deep cream and a pea-sized amount deep golden brown, using brown with a touch of egg yellow. Model tiny teardrop shapes for hair and eyebrows. For arms, use just under 15g (½oz) of cream modelling paste, split into four equal pieces, and the step photograph as a modelling guide (see d). Stick the arms in place as each is made, bending into position and, if required, use foam pieces for support until completely dry.

**9** Using the remaining cream, model little sausage-shaped legs, making the eaten elfin's legs longer, pinching a knee half way on each. Colour 45g (1½oz) of modelling paste brown. Split 22g (¾oz) into six equal sized pieces. To make a shoe, first roll a long teardrop shape and pinch up at the full end. Hollow this out slightly by pinching up a rim. Mark little pleats, using a cocktail stick, and indent by pinching underneath to shape the arch of the foot. Make

all the shoes and stick in place as each are made.

## Backpacks

**10** To make a backpack (see e), shape 7g (¼oz) of brown modelling paste into a teardrop. Press down onto the pointed end to indent, pushing up excess either side. Pinch this excess up, twist each to a point and wrap around the end of a backpack twig. Thinly roll out the remaining brown for mats and, using the knife, score two oblong shapes measuring 5 x 8cm (2 x 3in) on the surface. Carefully tear out the oblong shapes – this will create a ragged edge but keep neat lines. Fold one over and roll up another and stick in position on the cake board. With trimmings, make some more twigs for the fire.

**11** Colour 7g (¼oz) of modelling paste pale brown and, using the remaining dark cream, make two further backpacks as before.

## Camp fire

**12** For the fire, colour the remaining modelling paste egg yellow, kneading until streaky, then shape into a teardrop. Cut into the pointed end with a knife to shape flames and pull each up, tearing off the excess paste. Stick the flames in position on the centre of the fire twigs.

## Magical touches

**13** Mix dark green and egg yellow powder food colourings separately with a little icing (powdered) sugar. Brush green colour around the cake board and rocks, and egg yellow colour around the surrounding area of the fire to create fire glow. Brush the whole cake with edible sparkle powder.

d

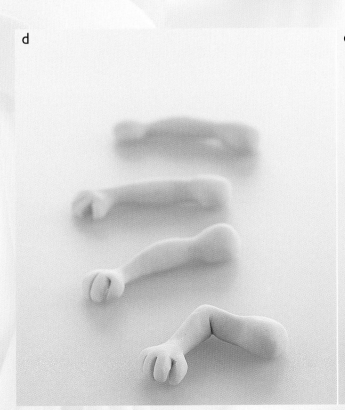

e

# Emerald City

I made lots of jewel-coloured fairies to show how different they all could be, but choosing just one jewel in a birthstone colour would beautifully personalize this cake.

## Cake & decoration

(See pages 7–13 for recipes and cake chart)
3 x 15cm (6in) round cakes
25cm (10in) round cake board
1.875kg (3¾lb) sugarpaste (rolled fondant)
Mint green, red, blue, violet, egg yellow, golden brown, brown and black food colouring pastes
440g (14oz/1¾ cups) buttercream
Icing (powdered) sugar in a shaker
Sugar glue
75g (2½oz) modelling paste
12 sugar sticks
Green, red, blue, violet, silver, gold and clear green edible glitters
90g (3oz) royal icing

## Equipment

Large rolling pin
Serrated and plain kitchen knives
Miniature and 5cm (2in) circle cutters
Length of thread
Ruler
Cake smoother
Templates (see page 93)
A few cocktail sticks
Small daisy and star cutters
6 paper piping bags
Fine and medium paintbrushes
Pieces of foam sponge

## Cake board and cake

**1** Colour the sugarpaste (rolled fondant) green. Roll out 315g (10oz) and cover the board. Press the rolling pin into the surface to indent ridges. Trim excess from around the edge, then put aside to dry. Trim the crust from each cake and slice the tops flat. Cut a layer in two of the round cakes and sandwich all four layers together with buttercream. Cut out four circles from the third cake, using the 5cm (2in) circle cutter. Sandwich together to make the two towers, trimming each to a total height of 12cm (5in) (see a). Spread buttercream over the surface of the cakes.

**2** Roll out 100g (3½oz) of green sugarpaste and place the top of the large cake down onto it. Cut around, lift and put back on its base. Measure around the cake, using the length of thread, and cut to size. Measure the depth of the cake with a ruler. Roll out

a

410g (13oz) of green and cut an oblong using these measurements. Sprinkle with icing sugar to prevent sticking, roll up from one end, position against the cake and unroll around the sides *(see b)*. Trim excess from join and glue together. To remove the join completely, rub gently with a little icing sugar. Position the cake on the cake board, slightly towards the back, and rub the surface with a cake smoother. Cover the two tower cakes in the same way using 315g (10oz) of green sugarpaste.

**3** To make the structural wall for the large cake, roll out 410g (13oz) of green sugarpaste and cut an oblong measuring 38x20cm

(15x8in). Measure 14cm (5½in) from the bottom on the left-hand side and cut at an angle straight across to the top corner on the right-hand side. Moisten the cake with sugar glue, place the shortest side against the front and smooth around the cake. The highest point at the back will be a little floppy at first: just keep smoothing it back into place until it begins to firm. If the edges are uneven, use a cake smoother to push them back.

**4** Using the template (see page 93), cut out a doorway in the front, removing the structural wall piece only. Thinly roll out this piece of paste and cut out the door. Stick in position and mark holes using the tip of a cocktail stick (tooth-pick). Roll out trimmings and cut two strips for steps, the bottom step slightly thicker than the top. Model a small door handle.

**5** Using the remaining green sugarpaste, make the walls for the two towers, using the template

(see page 93), and stick in place as before. Using a knife, mark crosses for windows and indent into each corner with the end of a paint-brush *(see c)*. Using sugar glue, stick each tower in position, checking that the top tower is sitting completely straight.

## Fairies

**6** Each fairy is built up flat until the hair is piped. Colour 15g (½oz) of modelling paste green, and then 7g (¼oz) each for red, blue, violet and egg yellow, with 7g (¼oz) white. Put aside half of the green until later.

**7** To make a fairy *(see d)*, split the respective coloured modelling paste in half and use one half to shape the dress. First, model a teardrop shape and press to flatten slightly. Indent radiating lines using the paintbrush handle and smooth along the bottom to thin and frill. With the remaining half, roll out and cut a collar and crown using the daisy cutter, then cover

b

c

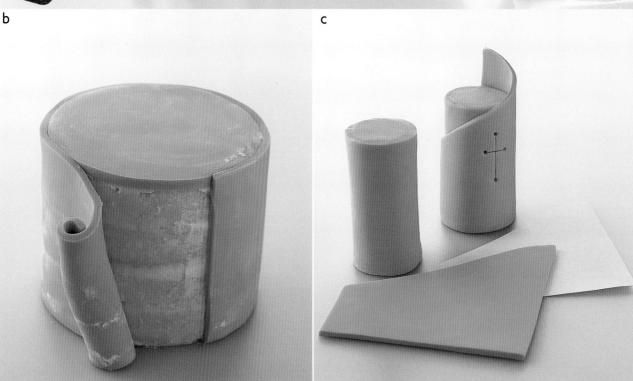

to prevent drying. Cut a star and stick to the top of a sugar stick to make the wand. Model the remainder into four teardrop shapes for wings, with two slightly larger, and press flat.

8 Paint sugar glue over the bottom of each fairy's dress, wings, crown and wand, and sprinkle with glitter. Split 22g (¾oz) of modelling paste into six equally sized pieces. Colour each a different skin tone using golden brown and brown food colouring pastes. Split each piece in half and roll into a ball-shaped head. Indent a smile using the miniature circle cutter, pressed in at an angle, then dimple the corners using the tip of a cocktail stick. Model a tiny ball nose for each.

9 Using the remaining skin tone modelling paste, make two legs and two arms with each shade. To make a leg, roll the paste into a thin sausage and bend one end round to shape the foot. Pinch out a heel at the back and press either side of the foot to narrow and lengthen. Pinch gently underneath to indent the arch of the foot. Pinch around the ankle and then stick in position.

10 To make an arm, roll the paste into a thin sausage, rounding off one end for the hand. Press the hand to flatten slightly and then stick the arms in place with the collar on top. Push a sugar stick down through the dress, leaving a little protruding to help hold the head in place. Make a small hole in the base of each head, using a cocktail stick, and press onto the sugar stick, securing at the base of the head with a little sugar glue.

11 Stick each fairy in place on the castle, using dabs of royal icing. Hold each for a few moments until secure. Split the royal icing into six and colour light blonde and dark blonde using a touch of egg yellow food colouring paste, pale golden brown, and the remaining three different shades of brown. Put the coloured icings into piping bags and cut a small hole in the tip. Pipe the hair by waving the bag gently from side to side to create waves and curls, then place on their crowns. Stick the fairies' wands in place.

## Magical touches

12 Using the remaining green modelling paste, roll into balls and roll in green glitter while they are soft, so the glitter will stick to the surface (see e). Stick together in groups of three and use to decorate around the top edges. Finally, brush a tiny amount of the clear green glitter all over the cake.

13 When the cake is dry, dilute black food colouring paste with a little water and carefully paint the eyes on the fairies using the fine paintbrush.

d

e

# Ramshackle Village

A little cobbled street where trolls live in odd dwellings, all misshapen and rickety, is the last place where you would expect to find treasure. But that is exactly why it's buried there!

## Cake & decoration

(See pages 7–13 for recipes and cake chart)
25cm (10in) square cake
30cm (12in) hexagonal cake board
1.65kg (3lb 5oz) sugarpaste
(rolled fondant)
Cream, black, brown and chestnut
food colouring pastes
Icing (powdered) sugar in a shaker
345g (11oz) modelling paste
440g (14oz/1¾ cups) buttercream
Sugar glue
2 sugar sticks
Edible gold glitter
Edible gold powder

## Equipment

Large and small rolling pins
Plain and serrated kitchen
knives
Ruler
Sheet of card for templates
Templates (see page 94)
Small glue brush
Medium paintbrush
A few cocktail sticks
2.5cm (1in) square cutter
1.5cm (¾in) circle cutter
Pieces of foam sponge
Dusting brush

## Cake board

1 Colour 1.09kg (2lb 3oz) of sugarpaste (rolled fondant) stone using cream colouring paste with a touch of black. Roll out 375g (12oz) and cover the board, trimming excess from the edge. Cut templates 1cm (½in) larger than the base of each house (see cutting diagram on page 95) and position on the cake board. Score around the front of each as a guide for the cobbles. Trim out a little hole at the front of the cake board. Colour 60g (2oz) of sugarpaste black and fill, using a small piece (see a). Using stone sugarpaste trimmings, model piles and group around the hole. Model a large pile, then chop up some more trimmings into small crumbs and put aside. Colour 60g (2oz) of modelling paste dull brown using brown and black food colouring pastes, 155g (5oz) brown and 60g (2oz) chestnut brown. To make the cobbles, roll out 45g (1½oz) of each and cut into squares. Stick onto the

a

cake board, following the guiding lines. Reserve some cobbles to edge around each house.

## Dwellings

**2** Trim the cake crust and slice the top flat. Using the cutting diagram (see page 95), cut out the shapes to assemble the dwellings. To assemble the largest dwelling, put the three larger squares, one on top of the other. Trim the slanted roof shape equally either side, cutting down and taking off the top edge of the second layer. Trim the front and back of the house to slope inwards. For the medium dwelling, put the 8x7cm (3x2¾in) cake on top of the 7x6.5cm (2¾x2½in). Trim either side at the top and then turn one trimming over and use to give height and create the angled roof. The small oblong dwelling is turned upright with an angled roof trimmed. Trim down each side to curve slightly inwards.

**3** Sandwich all layers together with buttercream, then spread a layer over the surface of each cake to help the sugarpaste stick. Colour 500g (1lb) of sugarpaste dull brown using brown and black food colouring pastes. With 15g (½oz), pad the top of each roof at either end. Thinly roll out black sugarpaste and cover the window and door areas (see b). Using 625g (1¼lb) of stone sugarpaste, cover all sides of the two large houses by rolling out and placing the sides down onto it and cut around. Close joins with sugar glue, then rub gently with a little icing sugar to remove completely. For the smallest dwelling, roll out a strip to cover around all sides and close the join at the back. Mark little cracks and imperfections over the surface of all three cakes. Cut out all the misshapen doors and windows, exposing the black areas underneath.

**4** Roll out 170g (5½oz) of dull brown sugarpaste and cut a piece to cover the roof area on the largest cake. With 125g (4oz), cover the other two roofs the same way. Thinly roll out the remaining dull brown sugarpaste, a little at a time, and cut out 2.5cm (1in) squares for the roof tiles. Roll the handle of the paintbrush along the bottom edge of each to thin and frill. Build up over the roof, overlapping each layer (see c).

**5** Thinly roll out black sugarpaste and stick on patches for the dormer windows on the roof and front of the largest dwelling, and either side of the smallest. Thickly roll out 45g (1½oz) of stone sugarpaste even thicker at the top and cut the roof dormer using the template. With 15g (½oz), make the dormer for the front using the template. Split 7g (¼oz) of stone sugarpaste in half and make the two small dormers for the smallest house. Cover the top of each with roof tiles. With the remaining stone sugarpaste, model three chimneys, indenting the top to hollow out.

b

c

**6** For the shutters and doors *(see d)*, roll out 60g (2oz) of brown modelling paste and indent lines over the surface using a ruler. Scratch lines for wood grain using a cocktail stick (toothpick). Mark an outline for all the shutters and doors, and tear to create a ragged edge. Using 15g (½oz), model logs and twigs, and make the wooden spade using 7g (¼oz). To make the spiked club, roll a small sausage handle, then roll a ball. Indent a hole underneath and stick in the handle. Indent holes, using the end of a paintbrush, for the spikes.

## Trolls

**7** For the trolls *(see e)*, first colour 15g (½oz) of modelling paste stone, 22g (¾oz) cream and the remaining piece grey. For the shoes, split just under 7g (¼oz) of dull brown in half and model into teardrops. For the trousers, shape a flattened sausage with 7g (¼oz) of brown. Make a cut to separate legs, smoothing to remove ridges. Stick onto the shoes and lay the figure flat. Model a flattened circle, using just under 7g (¼oz) of stone for the top. Split 7g (¼oz) of stone paste in half and make two sleeves, hollowing out the end of each. Thinly roll out the remaining dull brown and, using the template for the costume (see page 94), score around the paste, then tear out the shape. Stick both pieces over the top of his body. Use a sugar stick to help hold the head in place.

**8** Roll a ball head using 7g (¼oz) of cream and pinch out a long nose. Mark a smile using the circle cutter, then dimple the corners using a cocktail stick. Smooth along the smile with the glue brush to open the mouth. With pea-sized amounts, make the two ears, indenting the centre by rolling the paintbrush handle into each. Model two tiny black oval eyes. Stick the spiked club in place.

**9** Make two hands (see page 81, step 12 and e). Curve the hand round and stick into the sleeve. Put the troll upright and support with foam. Roll out grey paste and cut strips of different lengths for hair. Stick over his head with the shorter lengths around his face. For the club spikes, model tiny teardrop shapes and stick into the holes, points facing outwards.

**10** Make the troll in the window with only one arm, made from grey paste, holding a long teardrop of cream paste in one hand. Stick his head in the window recess and make hair using chestnut paste. With grey trimmings, cut small strips for hinges on doors and shutters, indenting holes with a cocktail stick.

**11** Arrange remaining cobbles around each house and sprinkle the crumbs. Model the sack with dull brown paste and fill with gold glitter. Moisten the large cream pile and small teardrop in the window troll's hand with sugar glue and sprinkle with gold glitter. Brush the cake with gold powder.

d

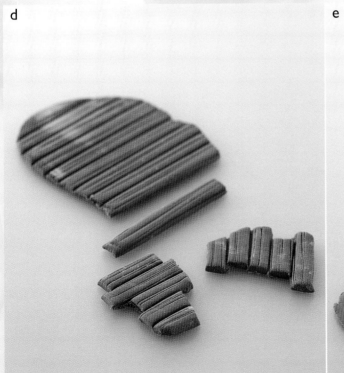

e

# King Neptune

I have always imagined King Neptune to have a kindly face and be a father figure to all the sea creatures, riding the waves with galloping seafoam horses in a chariot of shells.

## Cake & decoration

(See pages 7–13 for recipes and cake chart)

10cm (4in) and 20cm (8in) round cakes

30cm (12in) round cake board

410g (13oz) modelling paste

Icing (powdered) sugar in a shaker

280–300g (9–9½oz) royal icing

440g (14oz/1¾ cups) buttercream

1.25kg (2½lb) sugarpaste (rolled fondant)

Pink, navy, cream and black food colouring pastes

Sugar glue

Green and yellow powder food colourings

Confectioner's varnish or 2.5ml (½tsp) white vegetable fat

Edible gold sparkle powder

## Equipment

Plain and serrated kitchen knives

Large rolling pin

Small glue brush

Fine paintbrush

No. 4 plain piping tube (tip)

Template (see page 93)

Pieces of foam sponge

2–3 piping bags

Medium/large firm bristle paintbrush

Dusting brush

## Trident and carriage

**1** Make King Neptune's trident first, using 7g (¼oz) of modelling paste. Roll two-thirds into a sausage measuring 12cm (5in) for the handle. Shape the rest into a tapering sausage and bend into a horseshoe. Roll a long pointed centre and shape two flattened circles, one slightly larger. Assemble using royal icing, then leave to dry. Colour 7g (¼oz) of modelling paste pale pink. For the carriage base, knead half into 170g (5½oz) of white modelling paste until streaky, then roll into a long tapering sausage. Moisten along the length with sugar glue, then roll up into a spiral from the narrow end. Press down on the full end to create a seat area.

## Shells

**2** For shells (see a), knead a pea-sized amount of pink into 45g (1½oz) of modelling paste, leaving a little streaky, and split into seven pieces. To make a

a

shell, roll one piece into a teardrop shape and press down to flatten. Mark radiating lines with the paintbrush handle, then press either side to re-shape. Stroke out around the top edge to thin and frill. Cut the surface, using a knife held flat, and press underneath to curve round.

## Cake and cake board

**3** Trim the crust from each cake and slice the tops flat. Cut a layer in each cake, put one on top of the other and sandwich the layers with buttercream. To create waves, cut different-sized wedges from the top edge of both cakes, turn over and sandwich to the top surface (see b), protruding a little from the edge. Position the cake on the board and spread a layer of buttercream over the cake surface.

**4** Colour 1.25g (2½lb) of sugarpaste (rolled fondant) mid blue using navy colouring. Roll out and cover the cake and cake board completely, smoothing

around the shape, then pinch each wave, pulling gently downwards.

## Seafoam horses

**5** To make the seafoam horses, split 30g (1oz) of white modelling paste in half and make two teardrop-shaped bodies. To make the heads, split 22g (¾oz) of white and model into ball shapes, pinching out a muzzle on each. Cut smiles with the end of the piping tube, indenting the corners with the tip of a cocktail stick. Indent nostrils with the end of the paintbrush. Stick on tiny flattened circles for eyes and a tiny tapering sausage for each eyelid. For the ears, split a pea-sized amount into four and model into teardrops. Indent in the centre of each using the paintbrush handle. Cut the rounded end straight and position.

**6** For the horse legs, split 7g (¼oz) of white modelling paste in half and roll into sausages. Flatten the end of each and pinch half way to mark the knees. For

hooves, stick a pea-sized amount on the end of each, pinching to straighten the sides. Assemble on the cake (see c), sticking together with royal icing. Stick the carriage on top of the cake without the shell decoration.

## King Neptune

**7** Colour 90g (3oz) of modelling paste cream, putting just under 22g (¾oz) aside. To make King Neptune, roll the remainder into a tapering sausage and press down to flatten slightly. Pinch in a little at the waist and press either side to mark hipbones. Mark details on his torso using the paintbrush handle and a cocktail stick. Pinch at the top to shape a neck. Moisten the carriage with sugar glue and stick King Neptune on the seat, supported by the carriage. Mark scales on him using the No. 4 plain piping tube (tip), pressed at an angle over the surface.

**8** Roll a ball-shaped head with 7g (¼oz) of cream modelling

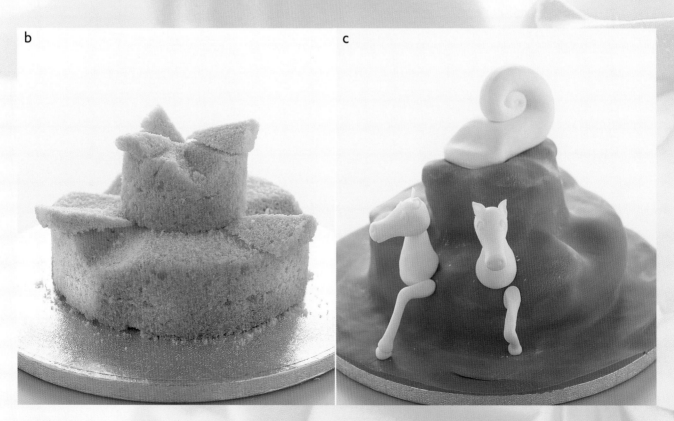

b      c

paste and using the step photograph as a guide (see d), stick on tiny facial details including two tiny flattened white pieces for eyes, and mark wrinkles and an open mouth using a cocktail stick. Stick onto the body with a generous amount of royal icing (none will show when the beard and hair are piped) and hold for a few moments until secure. For his crown, knead small amounts of pink and white together until marbled. Roll out and cut his crown using the template. Make cuts into each point, bend and stick onto the top of his head.

**9** Using pea-sized amounts of cream modelling paste for the tail fins, model each into flattened teardrop shapes. Press around the outside edge to thin and frill, then stick in place. For arms, split the remaining cream in half and, using the photograph as a modelling guide (see e), make two arms, one at a time, and stick them in place using pieces of foam sponge for

support. Stick the trident in King Neptune's hand.

**10** Colour 30g (1oz) of royal icing grey, mixing it until streaky. Put it into a piping bag and cut a small hole in the tip. Pipe King Neptune's beard, moving the piping bag from side to side to create waves. Pipe the moustache and the eyebrows, and finally the hair curling down his back with shorter curls framing his face.

**11** Pipe a thick line of white royal icing along the edge of each wave for foam. Dampen the firm paintbrush with water and draw the brush from the royal icing, diluting it and creating lines. Do the same effect around the tail fins. Paint the excess royal icing on the brush over the shell carriage and then stick all the shells in place using dabs of royal icing.

**12** Pipe large curls over the horses for their manes and for the sea foam around them.

Pipe extra foam along the edge of each wave. Roll four thin sausages of white modelling paste for reins and stick into the King's hands, with the ends attached to the back of each horse.

## Magical touches

**13** Dilute green and yellow powder colourings with a little icing (powdered) sugar. Brush green over the King's tail and fins, fading out with a little yellow. Brush the cake and trident with a little green colour.

**14** To give the sea a shiny effect, brush on 2–3 coats of confectioner's varnish, allowing each coat to dry for a few minutes before applying the next, or brush with a little white fat (shortening).

**15** Dilute black food colouring paste with a little water and paint the eyes using the fine paintbrush. To finish, randomly dust the whole cake with the edible gold sparkle powder.

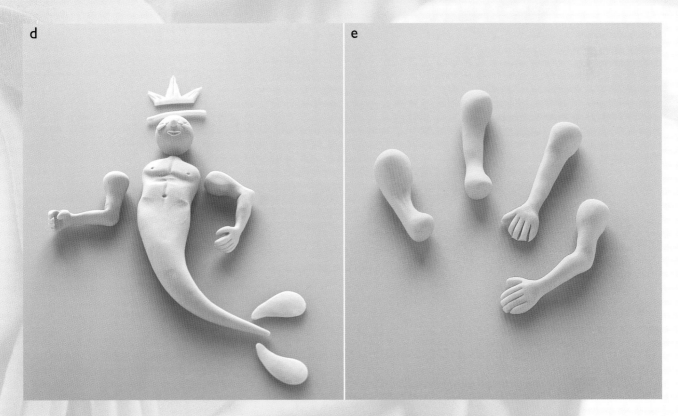

d

e

# Wizard Owl

White owls always look a little more mystical than others, so I made a snowy owl wizard reading spells from his chair of wisdom, which is made completely from books.

## Cake & decoration

(See pages 7–13 for recipes and cake chart)

25cm (10in) square cake
30cm (12in) round cake board
2kg (4lb) sugarpaste (rolled fondant)
Navy blue, chestnut, black and yellow food colouring pastes
Icing (powdered) sugar in a shaker
410g (13oz/1⅔ cups) buttercream
Sugar glue
315g (10oz) modelling paste
Edible gold powder

## Equipment

Large rolling pin
Plain and serrated kitchen knives
Ruler or similar straight edge
Cake smoother
Small glue brush
Medium paintbrush
A few cocktail sticks
Template (see page 93)
Pieces of foam sponge
1cm (½in) and 1.5cm (¾in) circle cutters
Dusting brush

## Cake board

1 Colour 375g (12oz) of sugarpaste (rolled fondant) navy blue and knead until streaky. Roll out and cover the cake board completely, trimming excess from around the edge, then put aside to dry.

2 Trim the crust from the cake and slice the top flat. Cut the cake (see a) as in the cutting diagram (see page 95). Take off 1cm (½in) from the depth of both owl layers and put them together. Trim to round the body shape and then sandwich the layers together with buttercream. Spread all the cakes with buttercream to help the sugarpaste stick.

## Chair of wisdom

3 Colour 1.5kg (3lb) of sugarpaste stone using a touch each of chestnut and black food colouring paste. Roll out 90g (3oz) and cut a strip to cover

a

around three sides of the seat book. Indent pages by pressing in with a ruler.

4 To make the book cover, measure the book, roll out 265g (8½oz) and cut an oblong to fit around the cake. Position the cake on the right-hand side of the rolled-out sugarpaste and flip over the left-hand side, pressing the cake smoother along the edge to straighten or trim any excess (see b). Smooth the binding until it curves round. Mark a line on the top by pressing in with a ruler. Position the cake centrally on the cake board.

5 Make two sugarpaste books, one for the seat and another for a support for the back of the chair. Thickly roll out 280g (9oz) of sugarpaste and cut two oblong shapes measuring 6 x 10cm (2½ x 4in). Mark pages as before around three sides of each. Roll out 170g (5½oz) and cut covers for both, slightly larger than the pages, then

wrap around the pages, sticking with sugar glue. Mark the binding as before, then set aside. Cover the cake for the chair back as previous instructions and position on top of the seat, level with the back, securing with sugar glue. Stick the two sugarpaste books in position on the chair.

6 With the remaining stone sugarpaste, cover the two cakes for the book arms in the same way and stick in position, leaning slightly inwards. Cut little cracks in the books using a knife. Roll out trimmings and cut strips for the binding on all books.

## Wizard Owl

7 Roll out the remaining white sugarpaste and cover the owl's body, smoothing the sugarpaste down and stretching out any pleats. Trim away excess sugarpaste from around the base of the body. Indent over the surface to mark feathers using the paintbrush handle (see c).

8 To make the head (see d), roll 125g (4oz) of modelling paste into a ball. Shape a flattened teardrop, using 22g (¾oz), and stick the point on the centre of the owl's face, then smooth up and over the top of his head. Pinch up ears either side and stroke the eyebrow area to lift and flatten slightly. Indent each eye area by pressing in with your finger.

9 Colour a pea-sized amount of modelling paste yellow, split into two and model two flattened circles for eyes. Use two pea-sized amounts to make eyebrows. Take care when positioning his eyebrows. Although he has quite a serious expression, if the eyebrows are positioned too low over his eyes, this will result in his face looking unfriendly. Split 7g (¼oz) of white in half and make the teardrop-shaped cheeks. Roll five small teardrop shapes and stick the points together for his beard. Using the paintbrush, mark lines to give texture around his eyes and

b

c

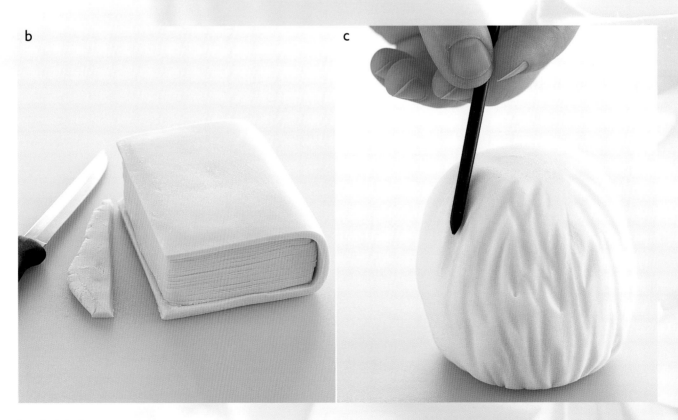

cheeks, and then stick the head onto the body.

## Cloak

**10** Colour 90g (3oz) of modelling paste navy blue. Thinly roll out 60g (2oz) and cut a cloak, using the template (see page 93). Roll the paintbrush over the surface to create pleats, and then stick around the owl's shoulders. Lift the owl and stick him in position on his chair. Slot a small piece of foam either side of the cloak to hold it open ready for the wings.

## Scroll and wings

**11** For the scroll, thinly roll out 22g (¾oz) of white modelling paste and cut a strip measuring 4 x 15cm (1½ x 6in). Stick against the owl and chair, curling over at the top and rolling it up a little at the bottom. Split 30g (1oz) of modelling paste in half and, using the step photograph as a guide (see e), make the two wings, marking feathers along the

bottom edge with the paintbrush handle. Carefully slot the wings in position on the body, securing them with sugar glue.

## Hat and face

**12** To make the Wizard Owl's hat, roll the remaining navy blue modelling paste into a teardrop shape and pinch out a rim around the full end. Stick on top of his head, twisting up the point. Model two tiny dots of white for the eye highlights and put aside.

**13** Colour the remaining modelling paste black. For his beak, model two teardrop shapes using pea-sized amounts. Indent into one for the bottom part of the beak. Stick them together, then stick onto the owl's face and stroke downwards slightly. Edge around each eye with very thin uneven sausages of black and model two flattened circles for pupils. Stick the highlights in the same position on each eye.

## Glasses

**14** Roll out the remaining black modelling paste and cut out two circles using the larger circle cutter. To make hoops for the glasses frame, cut out another circle from the centre of each using the smaller cutter. Leave to set for a few moments and then stick each hoop in place against his beak and cheeks. Roll long pointed claws using the black modelling paste trimmings, bend them to shape and stick in place.

## Magical touches

**15** Paint stars with sugar glue over the hat and cake board, a few at a time. When they are tacky, brush with the edible gold powder. When the cake is completely dry, brush more gold powder randomly over the cake and cake board using the dusting brush.

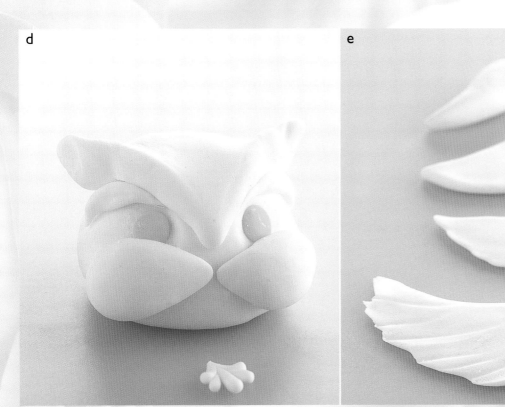

d

e

# Labyrinth

With its towers, tunnels, secret doors and a maze of walkways, these cute little brightly coloured gnomes must be dizzy trying to find their way to the castle in the centre.

## Cake & decoration

(See pages 7–13 for recipes and cake chart)

25cm (10in) square cake

35cm (14in) square cake board

2kg (4lb) sugarpaste (rolled fondant)

Cream, black, brown, violet, blue, raspberry and green food colouring pastes

845g (1lb 11oz) modelling paste

440g (14oz/1¾ cups) buttercream

Icing (powdered) sugar in a shaker

Sugar glue

6 sugar sticks

Lilac powder food colouring

## Equipment

Large and small rolling pins

Plain and serrated kitchen knives

Fine paintbrush

Small glue brush

Miniature and 1.5cm (¾in) circle cutters

2.5cm (1in) square cutter

A few cocktail sticks

Pieces of foam sponge

Dusting brush

## Cake board and towers

1 Colour 750g (1½lb) of sugarpaste (rolled fondant) dark cream. Roll out 500g (1lb) and cover the cake board completely, then trim excess from around the edge. Using your hands, mark an uneven surface, then put aside to dry.

2 Colour 440g (14oz) of modelling paste pale cream and use to model all the towers (see a). They are all shaped from a sausage shape that tapers at one end with both ends cut straight. The large central tower on top of the cake is 100g (3½oz). The three surrounding ones are 30g (1oz) for one and 15g (½oz) each for the remaining two. Shape a small square tower using 22g (¾oz), cutting at an angle each side at the top for the sloping roof. Split the remaining pale cream paste into eight and model the towers around the outside wall. Indent windows using the paintbrush handle.

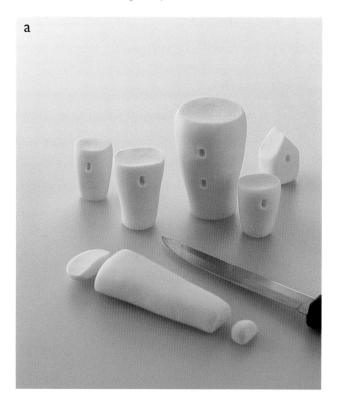

a

## Labyrinth

**3** Trim the crust from the cake and slice the top flat. Cut a 2.5cm (1in) strip from one side of the cake and cut this strip into three lengths. Sandwich together with buttercream to make the smaller square cake. Remove a further 2.5cm (1in) strip from the longest side of the larger cake to make it square. Cut a layer in the large square and sandwich back together with buttercream. Place centrally on the cake board. Spread a layer of buttercream over the surface of both cakes to help the sugarpaste stick.

**4** Roll out the remaining dark cream sugarpaste and cover the top of both square cakes, trimming excess from around the top edge. Place the small square cake centrally on top of the larger cake. Colour 1.25kg (2½lb) of sugarpaste pale cream. Roll out 875g (1¾lb) into a strip to fit around the large cake, measuring 8cm (3in) in depth. Dust with icing (powdered) sugar and roll up. Place one end against the large cake and unroll the sugarpaste around the cake, trimming away excess at the join (see b). To remove the join, stick together with sugar glue, and then rub gently to close. Cover the smaller square cake in the same way using 200g (6½oz), cutting the strip with a depth of 6cm (2½in).

**5** Cut out all the windows around the cake and on the cake board, using the round and square cutters. Colour sugarpaste trimmings black, thinly roll out and cut out shapes to fill each window (see c).

**6** Thickly roll out and cut strips measuring 2.5cm (1in) in height for the two walls on top of the large cake, using the remaining cream sugarpaste. Stick in position with gaps ready for the little doors, and on the inner wall and double gates at the front. Colour 60g (2oz) of modelling paste brown and use to make all the doors, shutters and gates, marking lines in the surface with the back of a knife for planks and using the blade to score a wood grain effect (see d). Using the cream trimmings, roll out and cut the doorsteps and strips to edge the windows and doors. Shape different-sized oval shapes and stick onto the surface of the labyrinth, pressing each flat. Colour 7g (¼oz) of modelling paste pale grey and model the sausage-shaped bars, indenting in the centre of each to narrow, and make all the hinges and door handles.

**7** Colour 75g (2½oz) each of modelling paste mauve and pale mauve using a touch each of violet and blue, and another 75g (2½oz) violet, then use to make all the tower roofs. Model into teardrop shapes first, then roll the point long and thin. Pinch around the full end to indent underneath and create an edge. Stick the wall tower roofs in place supported by the top edge of the wall.

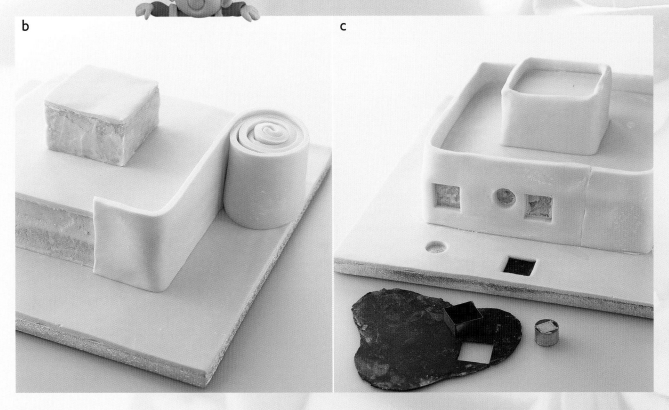

b

c

## Gnomes

**8** To make the gnomes (see e), first colour 7g (¼ oz) of modelling paste pale blue, 7g (¼ oz) deep violet, 15g (½ oz) raspberry, 15g (½ oz) green, 15g (½ oz) pale violet, 7g (¼ oz) deep cream and 22g (¾ oz) flesh, using cream food colouring paste with a tiny touch of raspberry. Each gnome is built up on the cake as each piece is made, all in different poses. The instructions that follow will make the gnome that is positioned at the front of the labyrinth, standing at the doorway.

**9** Using pea-sized amounts of pale blue, model oval shaped shoes first, pinching around the centre to narrow and press into the top to flatten ready for the trousers. Split the raspberry modelling paste into five pieces and shape one into a flattened square for trousers. Cut down the centre to separate the legs, smooth out all the ridges and then stick onto the shoes.

**10** Split the remaining white modelling paste into three pieces. Using one piece, make a top with two sausage-shaped sleeves, indenting into the end of each with the end of the paint-brush. Thinly roll out deep violet and cut two strips for braces, then stick a tiny green ball for a button onto the end of each, indenting in the centre with the end of the paintbrush. Push a sugar stick down through the top, leaving a little protruding to help hold the head in place. Split the flesh paste into seven pieces. Six are for all the heads, with the seventh making all the hands, noses and ears. Shape each head into an oval and stick lengthways over the sugar stick, securing at the base. Indent a smile using the miniature circle cutter pressed in at an angle, then dimple the corners using a cocktail stick (toothpick).

**11** To make the hat, split the green modelling paste into four pieces and shape one into a teardrop shape. Pinch up at the point to lengthen and indent into the full end to hollow out and pinch a rim. Model tiny oval shapes for the nose and two ears, then indent into each ear using the end of the paintbrush. For hands, split a pea-sized amount of flesh in half and shape into flattened teardrops. Cut a thumb on one side and two cuts along the top to separate three fingers on each, then stick into the sleeves. Using the remaining modelling paste, make all the other gnomes in various poses.

## Magical touches

**12** When the cake is dry, dilute a little black food colouring paste with water and paint the gnomes' eyes and tiny eyebrows using the fine paintbrush. Mix lilac powder colouring with some icing sugar and brush around the base of the cake.

d

e

# Pirate Dreams

Most children read under the covers with a torch and wonderful adventures are dreamed. For would-be swashbucklers, this ship-styled bed is afloat on a sea, flying the skull and crossbones.

## Cake & decoration

(See pages 7–13 for recipes and cake chart)
20cm (8in) square cake
35cm (14in) round cake board
625g (1¼lb) modelling paste
Dark brown, dark blue, red, black, cream, yellow and golden brown food colouring pastes
Icing (powdered) sugar in a shaker
315g (10oz/1¼ cups) buttercream
1.34kg (2lb 11oz) sugarpaste (rolled fondant)
Sugar glue
45g (1½oz) royal icing
Sugar stick
Yellow powder food colouring
Edible silver powder
Confectioner's varnish or white vegetable fat

## Equipment

Large and small rolling pins
Plain and serrated kitchen knives
Templates (see page 93)
1.5cm (¾in) and 2.5cm (1in) square cutters
Miniature and 1.5cm (¾in) circle cutters
A few cocktail sticks
Foam sheet and foam pieces
Bone tool
Fine and medium paintbrushes

## Headboard and bed

1 Colour 440g (14oz) of modelling paste brown. Roll out 155g (5oz) and cut the headboard and foot-board using the templates *(see a)*. Cut two circles from the footboard for the cannon holes. Thickly roll out another 155g (5oz) and cut four strips for the posts, measuring 15cm (6in) in length. Cut four squares from trimmings, using the smaller square cutter. Measure the side of the cake, roll out the remaining brown and cut two strips to fit the length, measuring 4cm (1½in) in height. Mark the wood grain by scratching the surface with a cocktail stick, then put to dry on a foam sheet. Roll a long sausage for the flagpole, using 7g (¼oz) of white modelling paste, and leave to dry.

2 Trim the crust from the cake and level the top. Cut the cake in half and put one on top of the other. Trim the two ends so they slope inwards towards

a

the base, then trim off the top edge around the cake. Sandwich the layers together with buttercream, then spread a layer over the surface to help the sugarpaste (rolled fondant) stick. Roll out 375g (12oz) of sugarpaste and cover the cake, trimming excess from the base. Colour 500g (1lb) of sugarpaste deep blue and roll out and cover the cake board, trimming excess from around the edge. Position the cake on the board. To indent a sea effect, mark the board with a bone tool and smooth ripples around each corner (see b). Make small dips where the bedposts will be.

**3** Stick the two bed sides against the base of the cake. Colour 235g (7½oz) of sugarpaste blue and 170g (5½oz) deep blue. Using 60g (2oz) of blue, model a pillow, pinching up four corners, and stick onto the bed, taking care not to go over the edge. Model another pillow with 60g (2oz) of white sugarpaste, indent in the centre

and mark pleats with the paintbrush handle. Thickly roll out the remaining blue and dark blue sugarpaste and cut squares using the larger square cutter. Pinch each square to soften the edges, then build up a chequered pattern to make the quilt (see c).

## Boy pirate

**4** Colour 30g (1oz) of modelling paste red. To make the pyjama bottoms, roll 22g (¾oz) into a fat sausage and press a little flat. Make a cut three-quarters of the length to separate legs, then smooth out ridges on either side. Flatten the end of each and pinch half way to shape the knees (see d). Bend and stick in position at the end of the bed. Roll out a little red, cut an oblong for the book cover and indent down the centre using the back of a knife. For pages, thickly roll out 7g (¼oz) of white paste and cut an oblong slightly smaller than the cover. Mark pages around the sides, indent down the centre and stick on the pillow.

**5** Colour the royal icing brown and use to stick the headboard and footboard in place with the posts. Shape just over 7g (¼oz) of white modelling paste into a teardrop shape for the pyjama top and indent around the full end to hollow out slightly. Press the point flat. Colour 45g (1½oz) of modelling paste black. Thinly roll out a little, cut a square, using the larger square cutter, and stick onto the pyjama top. Split 7g (¼oz) of black modelling paste in half and roll sausage-shaped sleeves. Bend half way and pinch out an elbow, then stick in position with one wrapped around the bedpost. Using a pea-sized amount of red, model a flattened circle for a collar and split another pea-sized amount to make two cuffs, indenting into the end of each with the end of a paintbrush. Model two pea-sized cuffs for the trousers, indenting as before. Push a sugar stick down into the body, leaving a little protruding to help hold the head in place.

b

c

**6** Colour 15g (½oz) modelling paste cream. Roll two-thirds into a ball-shaped head and press down onto the sugar stick, securing at the base with sugar glue. Mark the centre of the face using the tip of a cocktail stick (toothpick), and use as a guide for the mouth and eyes. Push the end of the paint-brush into the mouth and pull down slightly. Indent closed eyes using the miniature circle cutter pushed in at an angle. Mark tiny eyelashes in each corner and little eyebrows using the tip of a cocktail stick. Stick on a tiny ball nose and model two oval-shaped ears, indenting into the centre of each with the end of a paintbrush. Stick the ears in place. Colour 7g (¼oz) of modelling paste pale yellow and model different-sized flattened teardrops for the hair.

**7** Colour a marble-sized piece of modelling paste grey. Make the cutlass (see e) using the step photograph as a modelling guide. Rub with silver powder and then

set aside. Split the remaining cream modelling paste into four pieces, with two slightly larger, and make two hands and two feet. To make a foot, model a small sausage with a larger piece and pinch up an ankle, shaping the heel. Pinch in the centre to arch the foot and stick in place. For hands, see page 77, step 8. Pinch around the wrist and slot into the end of the sleeve, securing with glue. Wrap the fingers around the cutlass handle and secure against the bedpost. Using a pea-sized amount of red, make tassels.

**8** Colour 15g (½oz) modelling paste pale golden brown and make the teddy, using half for the teardrop-shaped body. Model a little red flattened circle for the collar and teardrop-shaped ties. Assemble him against the foot-board, sticking with dabs of royal icing. Roll out white and cut the waistcoat using the template. Use just over 7g (¼oz) of black to make both pirate hats, one larger than the other. Indent on the

underside so they sit neatly on the heads, then turn up the two ends. Model a tiny nose and eyes.

## Magical touches

**9** With the remaining black, model two cannons, three cannon balls and the torch. Roll out and cut a flag, using the template (see page 93). With black and red trimmings, model flattened circles for the top. Using the templates and the remaining white modelling paste, make all the skull and crossbones, smoothing the paste into the surface to inlay. Stick the flagpole in place using royal icing. Dust radiating lines of yellow powder from the torch for the torchlight and rub silver powder onto the end of the torch. Paint 2–3 coats of confectioner's varnish over the cake board, leaving each coat to dry for a few moments before applying another or, alternatively, rub the surface with white fat. Dilute black colouring with a little water and paint lines over the book pages for the print.

d

e

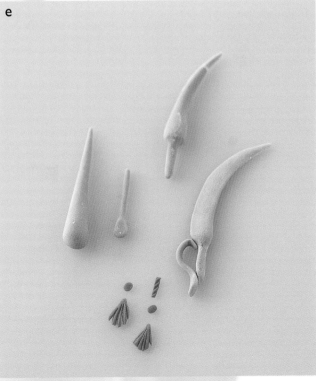

# Wizard's Helpers

I imagined how a wizard's table would look in the middle of the night and thought of these two naughty pranksters mixing potions. It is surprisingly simple to capture their cheeky looks.

## Cake & decoration

(See pages 7–13 for recipes and cake chart)
20cm (8in) square cake,
10cm (4in) and 15cm (6in) round cakes
30cm (12in) square cake board
1.75kg (3½lb) sugarpaste (rolled fondant)
Cream, black, mauve, brown, green and orange food colouring pastes
Icing (powdered) sugar in a shaker
440g (14oz/1¾ cups) buttercream
Sugar glue
280g (9oz) modelling paste
2 sugar sticks
15ml (1tbsp) clear piping gel
Edible gold powder
Edible gold glitter

## Equipment

Large rolling pin
Serrated and plain kitchen knives
6cm (2½in), 4.5cm (1¾in) and 3.5cm (1¼in) circle cutters
Ruler or straight edge
Small glue brush
Ball or bone tool
Pieces of foam sponge
A few cocktail sticks
Templates (see page 94)
Medium and large sable paintbrushes

## Cake board and cake

1 Colour 500g (1lb) of sugarpaste (rolled fondant) stone using a touch each of cream and black paste. Roll out 440g (14oz) and cover the cake board. Press the rolling pin and your hands over the surface to create ridges. Trim excess from around the edge, reserve trimmings, then set aside to dry. Trim the crust from each cake and slice the tops flat. Cut a 5cm (2in) strip from the square cake; the resulting oblong cake will make the book. Cut a layer in this oblong cake and sandwich back together with buttercream. For the hat, put the smaller round cake on top of the larger, with the 6cm (2½in) circle cutter centrally on the top. Trim down the sides from the circle cutter to the edge of the base of the large cake, creating the smooth sloping sides of the hat. Sandwich using buttercream, then spread a layer over the surface of all the cakes (see a). Colour 750g (1½lb) of sugarpaste pale mauve. To give

a

height to the hat and help create the pointed top, model a teardrop shape of sugarpaste, using 75g (2½oz) of pale mauve, and press the full end onto the top of the hat, smoothing down around the join until it is level with the cake surface.

## Book

2 Roll out the remaining stone sugarpaste and cut a strip to cover around three sides of the oblong cake. Using the ruler or straight edge, mark lines to create the book pages, then pinch an edge at each corner. Colour 500g (1lb) of sugarpaste pale brown and roll out. Spread a little buttercream on the underside of the oblong cake and place down on the front of the rolled-out sugarpaste, leaving an exposed edge (see b). Trim to fit at least 38cm (15in) in length, then immediately flip the remaining sugarpaste over the top of the cake. Position the cake on the cake board. This may disturb the sugarpaste covering, so press the length

of the ruler against the edges to re-straighten or carefully re-trim any excess. Press down to mark a line for the binding using the length of the ruler and move gently backwards and forwards to flatten either side of the marked line. Roll out trimmings and cut two thin strips for the binding and stick in place with sugar glue.

## Wizard's hat

3 The hat covering and rim are made separately. To cover the hat, roll out 500g (1lb) of pale mauve sugarpaste and dust with icing sugar before rolling up. Position the sugarpaste against the side of the cake with excess at the top, then unroll around the cake, covering it completely. Trim excess from the join at the side and base. Smooth up the excess at the top and mould into the pointed top part of the hat (see c), tapering it to a point and securing at the side with a little sugar glue. Glue, press the join closed and rub gently with a little icing sugar to remove the

join completely. Secure the hat cake on top of the book cake using a little buttercream or sugar glue.

4 Roll out the remaining pale mauve sugarpaste into a circle measuring 20cm (8in). Cut away a circle from the centre, leaving a hat rim measuring 5cm (2in). Moisten around the base of the hat with sugar glue, then lift the hat rim over the top of the cake and secure at the base. To make the hatband, thinly roll out the trimmings and cut a strip measuring 41 x 2.5cm (16 x 1in). Cut the hatband along both sides at an angle, making a ragged edge, and stick around the base of the hat, crossing it over at the back.

## Bottles

5 Colour 100g (3½oz) of modelling paste grey and 60g (2oz) green. Use 45g (1½oz) of grey to make the spilt bottle. Model a small ball and press into the centre with a ball or bone tool to indent, making the bottle rim.

b

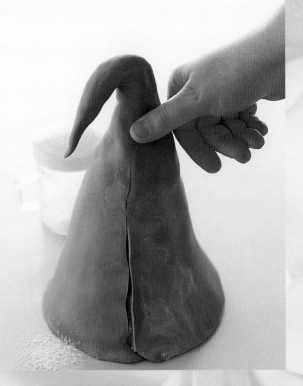

c

Roll the remainder into a ball and stick on the rim, and then stick the bottle in place on its side, up against the book. With just under 15g (½oz) of green modelling paste, roll into a sausage, tapering at either end. Pinch in the centre to pull up a little to fill the pot opening, smoothing the lengths unevenly against the cake board surface. With pea-sized amounts, model little teardrop splashes, sticking one onto the bottle rim with the others pressed on the cake board. For the large green bottle, shape the remaining green modelling paste into a ball and pinch gently to indent the neck of the bottle, keeping a rounded top. Press the ball or bone tool into the top to open it up, creating the rim. To make the little dish, colour 15g (½oz) of modelling paste orange and roll just under 7g (¼oz) into a ball. Press in the centre with your finger to indent and smooth round in a circular motion for a dip, then stick in position on the book cake.

## Imps

**6** Colour 45g (1½oz) of modelling paste brown and just over 7g (¼oz) mauve. Each imp is built up in place on the cake (see d for modelled shapes). To make the trousers for the first imp at the front, roll the remaining orange into a sausage shape, keeping the centre part fuller. Bend the two ends forward to make the legs, pinching gently to shape each knee, then pinch up the centre, smoothing the front flat. Stick onto the spilt bottle using small pieces of foam sponge to support each leg while drying. For the second imp, use the mauve paste and shape as before. Stick in place on the book, supporting with foam sponge between the legs until dry.

**7** For the tunic, shape 7g (¼oz) of brown modelling paste into a teardrop and cut the top and bottom flat. Mark a line down the centre and crease lines with a knife. Push in gently to indent the arm sockets either side at the top.

Using trimmings, thinly roll out and cut a tiny square pocket, indenting tiny stitches with the tip of a cocktail stick (toothpick), then shape three tiny flattened circular buttons. Push gently on the underside to indent, then stick the tunic onto the legs. Repeat for the second imp.

**8** Colour 7g (¼oz) of modelling paste stone as before and split into four pieces. Roll into sausage shapes, slightly narrower at one end, making the sleeves. Indent into each end to hollow out. Bend each half way, marking elbows, and stick in place using foam pieces for support. For each collar, split 7g (¼oz) of brown in half, shape two flattened circles and stick in place. To help support their heads, push a sugar stick down through each collar, leaving 2cm (¾in) pro-truding. For their shoes, split just under 7g (¼oz) of brown into four pieces and model each into a long

d

e

teardrop. At the full end, pinch around the top to shape an ankle and heel. Roll out pea-sized amounts of brown and cut out the top part using the template (see page 94). Stick the shoes in place with the top wrapped around and joining the leg to the shoe, using foam for support.

**9** Colour 30g (1oz) of modelling paste pale green and a minute piece black. Roll 7g (¼oz) of pale green into a ball-shaped head (see e) and pinch out a long nose, curving it downwards slightly. For the mouth area, thinly roll out a tiny piece of brown paste and stick just underneath the nose. The chin and bottom lip are tiny pale green sausages, each tapering to points at either end. Curve around and stick in place, edging the mouth area, and use the glue brush with a little sugar glue to blend each end in line with the surface. Roll a tiny pale green tapering sausage for the top lip and make two even smaller to shape the top of each eye. With

the tip of a knife, mark wrinkles at the corner of each eye. Split a pea-sized amount in half and shape into teardrop shapes for the cheeks, again smoothing in the points using the glue brush. With black, roll two minute tapering sausages for each eye then, using a cocktail stick, pull down a little, making the pupils. Make the second head as before.

**10** Split the remaining brown in half and model tear-drop-shaped hats, hollowing out each full end so they sit comfortably. For the ears, roll four pea-sized amounts of pale green into long teardrop shapes and indent down the centre with the ball or bone tool. Stick in place with each pointing outwards. Push each head down onto the sugar stick and secure with sugar glue.

**11** Split the remaining pale green into four pea-sized pieces. To make hands, model teardrops and press flat. Cut thumbs to the side at the pointed

end, then cut twice and twist to make three fingers. Pinch wrists and stick into the sleeves.

## Magical touches

**12** Roll out the remaining grey paste and cut two circles using the 4.5cm (1¾in) circle cutter (see f). From the centres, cut out circles using the 3.5cm (1¼in) circle cutter, and use the hoops for the frames. Cut a 4cm (1½in) strip, bend round and cut each end to join the frames. Stick on the board. Using the template, cut out the frame arms and position.

**13** Fill the dish and top of the bottle with piping gel, creating some drips on the rim and over the cake and board. Sprinkle a little glitter over the gel. Paint stars over the hat with sugar glue and, when tacky, brush on gold powder (see g). Paint glue onto the book corners and brush with gold. Edge with tack holes, indented with the tip of a cocktail stick. Brush gold over the cake and board.

f

g

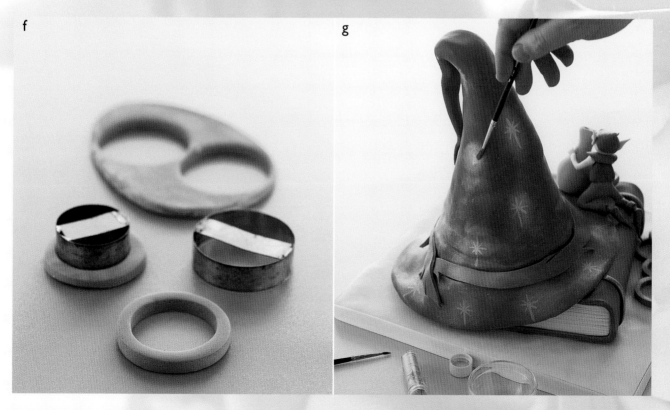

# Baby Dragon

Although this cake was initially made with smaller children in mind, anyone would fall in love with this baby dragon's cute expression and big blue eyes.

## Cake & decoration

(See pages 7–13 for recipes and cake chart)
3 x 625ml (1¼ pint/3 cup) bowl-shaped cakes
35cm (14in) round cake board
1.875kg (3¾lb) sugarpaste (rolled fondant)
Mauve, blue, black and green food colouring pastes
Icing (powdered) sugar in a shaker
315g (10oz/1¼ cups) buttercream
Sugar glue
Edible mauve sparkle powder
Edible purple glitter

## Equipment

Large rolling pin
Plain and serrated kitchen knives
Ball or bone tool
Small glue brush
Paintbrush
A few cocktail sticks
Pieces of foam sponge
Dusting brush

**1** Colour 625g (1¼lb) of sugarpaste (rolled fondant) pale mauve. Roll out 500g (1lb) and cover the cake board completely. Press the rolling pin over the surface to create ripples, then trim excess from around the edge and put aside to dry. Trim the crust from each cake and slice the tops flat. Cut a layer in one of the larger cakes, sandwich back together with buttercream, then place centrally on the cake board for the dragon's body. Trim the second larger cake to make the rounded end a little more pointed for the large eggshell. Spread a layer of buttercream over the surface of all the cakes to help the sugarpaste stick.

## Eggshells

**2** Roll out the remaining pale mauve and place the two eggshell cakes down onto it. Cut around, covering the top of each. Colour 500g (1lb) of sugarpaste blue. Roll out 315g (10oz) and cover the largest eggshell cake (see a). Leave 2.5–4cm (1–1½in)

a

excess around the edge, lift and put on its side. Cut a ragged edge, smoothing the points down towards the inside. Cover the smaller eggshell cake in the same way using the remaining blue. Reserve some of the pieces cut from the edge of the eggshell to decorate the cake board. With trimmings, shape different-sized flattened ovals to decorate the outside of each. Cut cracks, using a knife, and put the shells aside.

## Baby dragon

**3** Colour a pea-sized amount of sugarpaste black and put aside for later with two pea-sized amounts of white sugarpaste. Colour the remaining sugarpaste green. Roll out 185g (6oz) and cover the dragon's body, trimming excess from around the edge. Using the knife, press around the bottom edge to tuck under. Shape the neck, using 60g (2oz). Roll a sausage, tapering to a point, for the tail using another 60g (2oz) and bend up. Stick both against the

dragon's body (see b). To make the head, roll 155g (5oz) of green sugarpaste into a ball and indent to round off the muzzle. Stick onto the neck with the head turned slightly. Indent the open mouth using the small end of a ball or bone tool. Using 7g (¼oz), model facial features. Make two pointed ears and two flattened oval-shaped eyelids, smoothing the centre of each to indent. Model a pointed horn for the muzzle, two eyebrows and two pea-sized nostrils, indenting the centre of each with the small end of a ball or bone tool, slightly off centre.

**4** Using 7g (¼oz) of green, model the point for the end of his tail. Make a small hole in the bottom and stick in place using sugar glue. Model different-sized flattened oval shapes for scales using 60g (2oz) of green. Stick all over his back, neck and tail, hiding the joins. Keep the larger scales central down his back, with smaller ones either side (see c). For eyes,

stick on two white flattened oval shapes; use blue trimmings for the iris and then finish with black pupils. To make the wings, split 30g (1oz) of green sugarpaste in half. Model a teardrop shape and, from the full end, pinch up a point. Pinch another point in the centre and then indent in the direction of each point, using the paintbrush handle. Make the second wing, stick in place and support until dry.

**5** Split the remaining green into four pieces. To make legs, roll sausages and indent in the centre. Press to flatten, then cut twice in one end to separate claws. To position the eggshell cakes, stick a back leg on the dragon first and bend, sticking the leg and foot together. Moisten the base of the foot with sugar glue, then stick the eggshell cake in place, holding until secure. Wedge some shell pieces underneath for support and scatter a few over the board. Brush the cake with mauve sparkle powder and sprinkle glitter onto the wings.

b

c

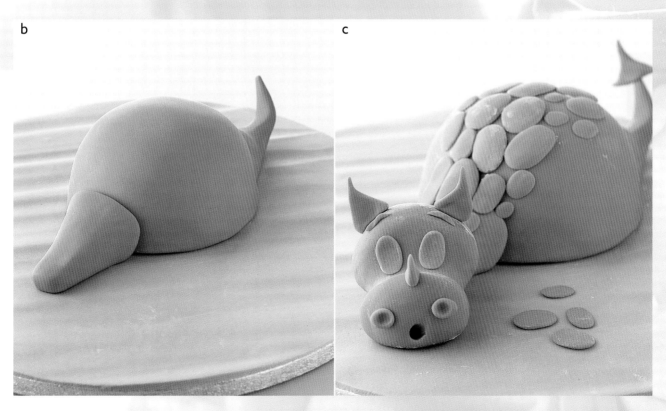

# Hocus Pocus

I just had to make three witches dancing around the cauldron as I have two sisters; so to me, these witches are called Debbie, Dawn and Jackie. Husbands are in the pot, of course!

## Cake & decoration

(See pages 7–13 for recipes and cake chart)

2 x 1 litre (2 pint/5 cup) bowl-shaped cakes

30cm (12in) petal-shaped cake board

1.17kg (2lb 5½oz) sugarpaste (rolled fondant)

Turquoise, yellow, mauve, black, green, cream, orange and blue food colouring pastes

Icing (powdered) sugar in a shaker

680g (1lb 5¾oz) modelling paste

280g (9oz/1 generous cup) buttercream

Sugar glue

Edible silver powder

## Equipment

Large rolling pin

Serrated and small/medium plain kitchen knives

Star cutters in various sizes

Small glue brush

Paintbrush

Template (see page 94)

A few cocktail sticks

Pieces of foam sponge

## Cake board and cake

**1** Split 375g (12oz) of sugarpaste (rolled fondant) into three pieces and colour turquoise, yellow and mauve. Knead the three colours together until streaky (see page 7). Roll out and cover the cake board completely, trimming excess from around the cake board edge. Cut out star shapes with the different-sized star cutters, removing the sugarpaste. Colour 60g (2oz) of modelling paste yellow and roll out to the same depth as the cake board covering. Cut out stars and slot into the spaces on the cake board (see a).

**2** Trim the crust from each cake and slice the tops flat. Slice a little off the bottom of each to create a flat area and then sandwich the two cakes together with buttercream to form the cauldron shape. Spread a layer of buttercream over the cake surface.

a

**3** Colour 750g (1½lb) of sugarpaste pale grey. Roll out and cut an oblong measuring 48 ×18 cm (19 × 7in). Dust with icing (powdered) sugar and roll up. Position against the cake, then unroll the sugarpaste around the cake *(see b)*, trimming excess from the join. To remove the join completely, moisten with sugar glue, then rub gently in a circular motion with icing sugar on your fingertips. Smooth around the top of the cauldron, creating a rim *(see c)*. For the silver effect, rub a little edible silver powder over the surface. Lift the cake and position centrally on the board.

**4** Colour 45g (1½oz) of sugarpaste green. To make the bubbling potion in the cauldron, roll 22g (¾oz) into five different-sized balls and position randomly inside the top. Roll out 15g (½oz) and cover completely, trimming excess. With the remainder, roll different-sized bubbles and scatter over the top.

## Witches

**5** To make the witches, first colour 140g (4½oz) of modelling paste mauve, 125g (4oz) green, 90g (3oz) cream, 60g (2oz) orange, 155g (5oz) blue and 22g (¾oz) pale blue. To make a dress, roll 90g (3oz) of mauve into a long teardrop shape and roll to flatten a little, keeping it slightly thicker at the narrow end. Mark pleats radiating down from the top using the paintbrush handle, then cut a ragged edge. Stick onto the side of the cauldron with the top level with the cauldron rim *(see d)*. For sleeves, split 15g (½oz) of mauve modelling paste in half and roll into long teardrop shapes. To open up each sleeve, push into the full end with your finger to indent and then pinch down the long tapering sleeve, rolling it gently between your fingers. Moisten at the shoulder and along the rim of the cauldron with sugar glue, then stick in place, holding until secure. Mark tiny stitches with the tip of a knife. With trimmings, cut a small square

pocket, stick in place and then mark stitches around the edge. To make the collar, roll a pea-sized amount of green modelling paste into a tapering sausage shape and stick around the top of the dress, crossing over at the front. Thinly roll out 7g (¼oz) of green and cut out a cloak using the template. Gently fold to create pleats and stick in place.

**6** For a head, roll 22g (¾oz) of cream modelling paste into a ball and gently pinch out a long nose. Just underneath the nose, draw a semi-circle for a mouth using a damp paintbrush. Move the brush backwards and forwards along the semi-circle, pushing in a little deeper each time. This will push out a rounded bottom lip. Stick the head in position, making sure it is well balanced and supported by the collar and the cauldron rim. Thinly roll out 15g (½oz) of orange modelling paste

b

c

for hair and cut into small strips measuring 2.5–4cm (1–1½in) in length. Build up the hair, leaving the top uncovered, finishing with smaller strips either side of her face. With orange trimmings, model minute flattened circles to decorate the dress patch.

**7** Press a 7g (¼oz) ball of blue paste flat and smooth around the edge to thin and frill, then stick onto the top of her head, making the hat rim. Roll 15g (½oz) of blue into a teardrop, tapering to a long point, then cut the full end straight. Stick onto the hat rim and bend the point around. To complete the hat, thinly roll out mauve modelling paste trimmings and cut a hatband.

**8** Roll a minute ball of cream paste and stick on a wart. For hands, split just under 7g (¼oz) of cream in half. With one half, shape a teardrop shape and press down to flatten. From the pointed end, cut a thumb on one side. At the point, make three cuts to separate

four fingers and twist each to a long point. At the full end, twist gently creating a long wrist, which will slot into a sleeve. Moisten inside a sleeve with sugar glue, then add the hand, holding until secure. Make a second hand, cutting a thumb on the opposite side.

**9** For the striped stockings (see e), twist pea-sized coloured sausages of modelling paste together, one pair orange and green, another mauve and green, and the last pair orange and blue. Make one stocking at a time. First, roll contrasting pea-sized amounts into sausages and stick together. To prevent cracking, moisten your hands slightly, then twist the sausages until the colours spiral. Roll gently to inlay, then taper each slightly at one end for the ankle.

**10** Using the remaining coloured modelling paste, make two more witches, spacing them evenly dancing around the cauldron. One witch has a blue

dress, orange collar and cloak, pale blue hair, purple hat and orange hatband, while the other has a green dress, mauve collar and cloak, blue hair, and orange hat with a pale blue hatband. Cut the cloaks in half, instead of folding, and position either side of each dress. The patches are left plain, with one indented with a tartan pattern using the back of a knife.

**11** Put a pea-sized amount of white modelling paste aside, then colour the rest black. Put aside a tiny amount of black for eyes, then split the remainder into six pieces to make all the shoes, following the step photograph as a guide (see e). Stick a stocking into the top of each and secure in position, using foam to support. Using white modelling paste, shape flattened oval shaped eyes and stick in position. Roll out and cut minute squares of white for teeth. With black, shape tiny flattened pupils and stick in place on the bottom of each eye.

d

e

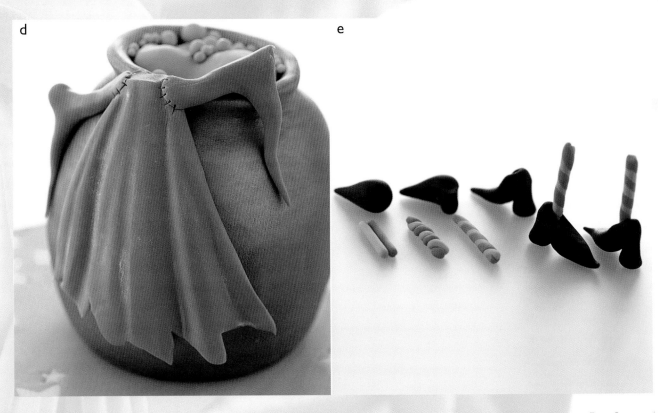

# Star Castle

A magical castle in the sky isn't complete without a pretty princess. I made her blonde with lots of curls, but she could be a look-alike for your very own little princess.

## Cake & decoration

(See pages 7–13 for recipes and cake chart)
25cm (10in) square cake
25cm (10in) round cake board
1.325kg (2lb 10½oz) sugarpaste (rolled fondant)
Blue, cream, yellow, black and red food colouring pastes
Icing (powdered) sugar in a shaker
440g (14oz/1¾ cups) buttercream
Sugar glue
170g (5½oz) modelling paste
10–15ml (2–3 tsp) royal icing
Edible silver paint

## Equipment

Large rolling pin
Plain and serrated kitchen knives
11cm (4½in), 8cm (3in) and 4cm (1½in) circle cutters
Length of thread
Ruler
Cake smoother
Small glue brush
2.5cm (1in) square piece of card
Fine and medium paintbrushes
Template (see page 93)
1.5cm (¾in) square cutter
A few cocktail sticks
Paper piping bag
Various star cutters

## Cake board and cake

**1** Knead a little blue colouring paste into 315g (10oz) of sugarpaste (rolled fondant) until streaky. Roll out and cover the cake board. Trim the crust from the cake and slice the top flat. Cut the cake exactly in half. From one half, cut two circles using the 11cm (4½in) circle cutter and sandwich together to make the base of the castle. From the remaining half, cut two 8cm (3in) circles and sandwich together for the second tier of the castle, and then two further circles measuring 4cm (1½in) for the third tier (see a). Cut a little from the depth of both small circles and sandwich together, making their total height 7cm (2¾in). Spread each cake with buttercream to help the sugarpaste stick.

**2** Colour 500g (1lb) of sugarpaste blue. To cover the top of the largest cake, roll out 75g (2½oz), place the top of the cake down onto it and cut around.

a

Measure around the cake, using the length of thread, and cut to size. Measure the depth of the cake and add another 1cm (½in). Roll out 410g (13oz) of blue sugarpaste and, using the two measurements, cut out the strip of sugarpaste to cover around the largest cake. Sprinkle with icing sugar to prevent sticking, roll up and place the sugarpaste against the side, and unroll around the cake (see b). Trim any excess from the join and stick together with sugar glue. To remove the join completely, sprinkle with icing sugar and rub gently with your fingertips. Create a smooth surface by rubbing gently with a cake smoother.

**3** Place the cake centrally on the cake board. Fold the card in half and push the fold into the covering to indent windows. Push the end of the paintbrush into the top and bottom of each. Cut out the doorway at the front using the template (see page 93). Smooth around the top with your fingertip.

Colour 7g (¼oz) of sugarpaste deep blue, thinly roll out and cut the door. Reserve the trimmings for later. Thickly roll out the remaining blue sugarpaste and cut a circle measuring 8cm (3in). Cut two steps, one larger, from the circle and assemble at the base of the doorway.

**4** For the second tier, colour 315g (10oz) of sugarpaste a slightly paler shade of blue than the bottom tier, and use 235g (7½oz) to cover the top and sides of the 8cm (3in) circle cakes as before. Stick centrally on the top of the bottom tier, making sure that the cake is level and sitting straight. For the dormer window at the front, thickly roll out 30g (1oz) and cut a 6cm (2½in) square. Cut another square from the centre and indent at each corner with the end of a paintbrush. Slice off the top at an angle to help shape the roof and stick in place. Thinly roll out the deep blue trimmings and cut a square to fill the window.

**5** Colour 100g (3½oz) of sugarpaste a paler shade of blue than the second tier. Roll out and cover the 4cm (1½in) circle cakes as before, marking a window at the front, and stick in place with sugar glue. For the fourth tier, colour 30g (1oz) of modelling paste palest blue and roll into a sausage. Cut the top and bottom straight, mark a small window using the tip of a knife, and stick in place. Check that all tiers are level and sitting straight.

### Towers and clouds

**6** To make all the towers (see c), roll the remaining pale blue sugarpaste into different-sized sausages, cutting the top and bottom of each straight. Cut the piece of card down to measure 1.5cm (¾in) square and mark a window in each as before. Colour the remaining sugarpaste mid blue. Thinly roll a tiny sausage and loop into the door handle, finishing with a tiny ball at the top. Roll out 7g (¼oz) and cut a strip for the roof

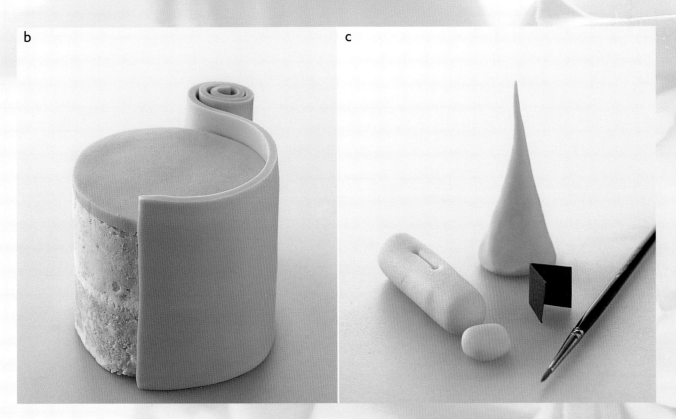

b

c

of the dormer window. Use the remaining mid blue sugarpaste to make all the different-sized roofs. Each roof is made from a teardrop shape, rolled with a tapering point and an edge pinched around the base which hollows out slightly underneath. The very top tower roof is made with 22g (¾oz). Stick the towers in place with a small ball of sugarpaste at the bottom, then stick a roof on top.

**7** For the clouds, roll 22g (¾oz) of white modelling paste into a sausage, tapering at either end, and roll over the surface to flatten slightly. Stick against the base of the castle and curve round on the cake board. Paint a line of sugar glue around the castle, where the long cloud will spiral round, and leave until tacky. Roll 45g (1½oz) of modelling paste into a thin tapering sausage, roll the surface as before, then carefully pick up and, following the glue line, press the edge of the rolled-out strip against it. Hold in place until secure.

## Princess

**8** Colour a marble-sized piece of modelling paste cream. To make the princess (see d), model her head, a tiny ball nose, her chest from a sausage with a pinched-up neck and two hands. To make hands, see page 41, step 11. Pinch around the wrist and then gently curve each hand round by pressing gently into each palm. Stick her head and chest area in place, holding for a moment. Colour 60g (2oz) of modelling paste pale blue. Split 7g (¼oz) in half and roll into a cone for her hat, cutting the bottom at an angle to fit around the back of her head. Stick in place onto her head, resting against the dormer window roof. To make the hat rim, roll a pea-sized amount of paste into a teardrop shape. Flatten, then cut in half and stick the pieces either side of her head.

**9** With the remaining piece, model one sleeve, pinching around the end to hollow out slightly for the hand to slot in

easily and roll down to a point. Make a tiny sausage for the top of her dress, pinching along the length to thin and frill. Stick one hand into the end of the sleeve, with the other resting against the window base. Colour royal icing pale yellow and, using the piping bag with a small hole cut into the tip, pipe curly hair by gently squeezing out the icing, waving the bag gently from side to side.

**10** Thinly roll out the remaining white modelling paste and cut a triangular hat scarf. Indent pleats by rolling the paintbrush handle over the surface and then stick in place. From the trimmings, cut a small square handkerchief. Roll out the remaining blue paste, cut out different-sized stars and stick around the cake and board. Paint the stars using edible silver paint (see e). When the cake is dry, dilute a little black and red paste separately with a little water, and paint her eyes and lips.

d

e

# Golden Pegasus

Magical Pegasus is the golden winged flying horse from Greek and Roman mythology. I have put him dancing amongst the clouds and stars in a sparkling, midnight blue sky.

## Cake & decoration

(See pages 7–13 for recipes and cake chart)
10cm (4in), 15cm (6in) and 20cm (8in) round cakes
35cm (14in) round cake board
1.75kg (3½lb) sugarpaste (rolled fondant)
Navy blue food colouring paste
Icing (powdered) sugar in a shaker
250g (8oz) modelling paste
Sugar glue
15g (½oz) royal icing
440g (14oz/1¾ cups) buttercream
Midnight blue sparkle powder
Edible gold powder
Edible gold glitter

## Equipment

Large rolling pin
Cake smoother
Plain and serrated kitchen knives
Small glue brush
Pieces of foam sponge
1cm (½in) circle cutter
Fine paintbrush
A few cocktail sticks
Template (see page 94)
Miniature star cutter
Kitchen paper
Dusting brush

## Cake board

**1** Colour 500g (1lb) of sugarpaste (rolled fondant) navy blue, roll out and cover the cake board. Rub the surface with a cake smoother. Trim excess from around the board edge and put aside to dry.

## Pegasus

**2** To allow drying time, make Pegasus first (see a). Using 45g (1½oz) of white modelling paste, shape his body flat on the work surface, twisting up a long neck and rounding off the rump. Smooth into the small of his back to create a dip, then gently push down to round off his underside and lift up his rump. As the paste is heavy, the back will flatten so, after a few moments, pick the body up and carefully reshape again.

**3** For legs, split 22g (¾oz) of white modelling paste into four pieces. To make a leg, roll one piece into

a

a sausage, fuller at the top for the thigh. Pinch around the bottom of the leg, rounding off the end. Bend the leg half way by pushing gently into the back to indent and pinch out a knee at the front. Stick in place with sugar glue immediately and smooth to blend into the surface of the body. To remove the join completely, rub gently in a circular motion with a little icing (powdered) sugar on your fingertips. Make three more legs in the same way, supporting each in their pose with pieces of foam sponge.

4 Model the head using 7g (¼oz) of white modelling paste. Roll into an oval shape first and, two-thirds down the length, roll backwards and forwards to indent and lengthen the muzzle, slightly rounding off the end. Stick in place using a dab of royal icing. Push the circle cutter in at an angle to mark the smile. Mark dimples in each corner and two nostrils, using the end of a paintbrush.

5 Stick on two tiny arched eyelids and flattened circles just underneath for eyes. Split a pea-sized amount of white in half and model teardrop shapes for ears. Indent in the centre of each using the end of a paintbrush and stick in place, pointing slightly outward at the top. Smooth the join closed.

6 Model four teardrop shapes for hooves using pea-sized amounts of white modelling paste for each. Stick the hooves onto the bottom of each leg, with the full part at the front. Press the front of each hoof to flatten.

## Cake

7 Trim the crust from each cake and slice the tops flat. Cut a layer in each cake and sandwich back together with buttercream. Spread a thin layer of buttercream over the surface of each cake to help the sugarpaste stick. Place the large cake centrally on the cake board. Roll out 625g (1¼lb) of

white sugarpaste and cover (see b), trimming excess from around the bottom edge. To obtain a smooth surface, rub gently with a cake smoother in a circular motion over the top and then smooth the sides. To create a smooth top edge, rub gently with the palm of your hand. Cover the remaining cakes on the work surface, using the remaining white sugarpaste. To stack each cake one on top of the other, carefully lift, holding at the bottom, and position centrally. Any finger-marks can then be smoothed away with the cake smoother.

8 Stick Pegasus to the bottom tier of the cake, using a few

b

c

dabs of royal icing, and hold for a few moments until secure. To prevent any slight sinkage that would damage the legs, wedge a piece of foam sponge between him and the cake board to hold in place until completely dry.

**9** Build up his mane and tail using different-sized sausages of white modelling paste, each tapering to a point. Keep the shorter lengths on top of his head and curl them up and around (see the main photograph as a guide to the mane and tail).

## Wings

**10** To make the wings (see c), thinly roll out 22g (¾oz) of modelling paste and, using the template (see page 94), cut out two wings. Thin and frill around the outside edge by making cuts on both sides, stretching them out and allowing some to break away. Model flattened teardrop-shaped feathers and stick in a line, following the outside shape of the

wing. Follow with two more lines, overlapping each on both wings. Carefully turn the wings over and attach more feathers on the reverse side. Stick the wings in place with a little royal icing, using pieces of foam sponge to support them while drying.

## Star and clouds

**11** Roll out 7g (¼oz) of white modelling paste and cut out all the stars, using the miniature star cutter, and put aside to dry.

**12** To make the clouds (see d), split the remaining white modelling paste into seven different-sized pieces. Each cloud is made from an oval shape first, which is then indented around the edge by pressing in with the paintbrush handle. Press down on the surface of each to flatten and rub around the edge to thin out. Put each cloud upright and bend in the centre slightly, so they will each follow the curved shape of the cake sides.

## Magical touches

**13** When the cakes are dry, protect the top of each cake with strips of kitchen paper and then dust a little midnight blue sparkle powder onto the sides of the cake, fading it out around the edge. Stick a cloud in front. Carefully remove the strips of kitchen paper and brush edible gold powder over the cake board in a spiral motion, to give a cloud effect. Stick the stars over the cake and cake board, positioning three stars upright on the centre of the top tier.

**14** Brush edible gold powder over all the stars and Pegasus (see e), concentrating more gold on his wings. Sprinkle a tiny amount of edible gold glitter over the cake and Pegasus. Dilute a little navy blue food colouring paste with water, then carefully paint his eyes, using the fine paintbrush. Take care not to have the paintbrush too wet to prevent the colour running.

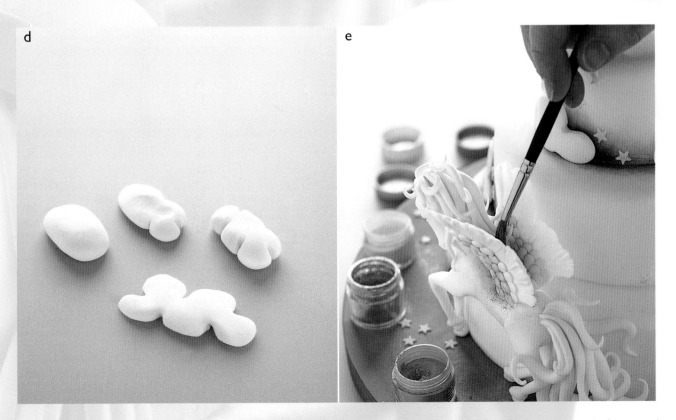

d

e

# Sprite Waterfall

As all children love playing with water, especially when splashing each other, I modelled these little sprites having a fun water fight in a pretty stone effect waterfall.

## Cake & decoration

(See pages 7–13 for recipes and cake chart)
10cm (4in) and 20cm (8in) round cakes
25cm (10in) round cake board
440g (14oz/1¾ cups) buttercream
1.25kg (2½lb) sugarpaste (rolled fondant)
Black, red, cream, purple, yellow, turquoise, golden brown and yellow food colouring pastes
Icing (powdered) sugar in a shaker
100g (3½oz) modelling paste
3 sugar sticks
Sugar glue
Apple green and orange edible pollen dusts
Edible gold powder
45–60ml (3–4tbsp) clear piping gel

## Equipment

Plain and serrated kitchen knives
Large rolling pin
Medium paintbrush
Small, medium and large star cutters
1cm (½in) circle cutter
Small glue brush
A few cocktail sticks
Pieces of foam sponge
Dusting brush

## Cake board and cake

1 Trim the crust from each cake and slice the tops flat. Cut a layer in each and sandwich back together with buttercream. Sandwich the two cakes one on top of the other and position on the cake board, leaving a space at the front (see a). Spread the surface of the cake with buttercream to help the sugarpaste (rolled fondant) stick.

2 Colour the sugarpaste pale grey using black food colouring paste. Roll out 875g (1¾lb) and cover the cake and cake board completely. Stretch out any pleats and smooth down and around the shape, trimming excess sugarpaste from the edge of the cake board. Mould the trimmings into two angular rocks for the top of the waterfall, one larger than the other, and indent the largest to create a well.

a

**3** Colour 15g (½oz) of grey sugarpaste a slightly deeper shade, 7g (¼oz) mid grey and 7g (¼oz) dark grey. To give the illusion of deep pools of water, thinly roll out and make the water shadows using the step photograph as a guide (see b), smoothing them to inlay level with the surface of the rock at the top of the waterfall and the cake covering. Using the paintbrush handle, mark lines at the waterfall of both cakes.

**4** Using the remaining grey sugarpaste, edge the waterfall with different-sized angular rocks (see c), marking ridges with the back of a knife. Model flattened pebbles for the cake board. To make white foam, roll tiny white sausages of modelling paste and roll along the length with the paintbrush handle to indent. Stick in position over the rocks at the bottom of each waterfall.

**5** Using 7g (¼oz) of white modelling paste, shape different-sized teardrop shapes for the base of each toadstool and stick in clusters around the cake. Colour 7g (¼oz) red and model the teardrop-shaped tops, hollowing out slightly underneath so they each sit neatly on their bases. Model tiny flattened circles of white for the spots.

## Sprites

**6** To make the sprites, first colour 30g (1oz) of modelling paste cream, 7g (¼oz) each of purple, yellow, turquoise, golden brown, a tiny amount black and another 7g (¼oz) green using yellow and turquoise food colouring. Make a sprite, one at a time, using the step photograph as a modelling guide (see d), and building up each figure in its pose on the cake.

**7** Just 7g (¼oz) of cream modelling paste is enough to model the legs, arms and head for one sprite, using half for the head, cheeks and eyebrows, with the other half, split into four pieces, for two arms and two legs. Use another 7g (¼oz), split into three pieces, for all three bodies. Make the legs first by modelling tapering sausages, bending half way to shape the knee. Model the body, pressing it a little flat, and stick on top of the legs.

**8** To make the costume, thinly roll out modelling paste and cut long tapering strips. From the full end, cut out a 'v' to give a ragged edge, then stick in place, layering around the body. Make the arms next from sausage shapes and pinch around one end to indent a wrist, rounding off the hand. Press down on the hand to flatten, then cut a thumb on one side, and three further cuts along the top to separate fingers. Pinch gently to remove ridges and lengthen slightly.

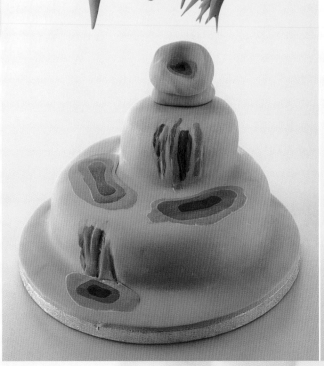

b

c

Bend the arm half way and pinch out an elbow at the back.

**9** Thinly roll out and cut a star collar, using the medium cutter, and cut repeatedly into the points to make ragged. Stick in place on top of the body, then push a sugar stick down through the body, leaving it half protruding to help support the head.

**10** To make a head, roll a ball and pinch out a pointed nose. Mark the smile, using the circle cutter pressed in at an angle, marking a semi-circle. Smooth the glue brush into the mouth and pull down for the bottom lip. Model teardrop-shaped cheeks, blending the point of each into the surface of the face using the glue brush. Model two eyebrows.

**11** To make wings (see e), thinly roll out the remaining white modelling paste and cut out three large stars. Cut each star in half to make one set of wings. From each

half, cut out triangles, leaving a neat star shape around the edge. Stick to the back of each sprite, using foam pieces for support until completely dry.

**12** For hair, thinly roll out modelling paste and cut a medium and small star. Cut repeatedly into the points, then stick onto the head with the small star on top and flick up a fringe. Colour a tiny piece of modelling paste black and make tiny oval-shaped eyes. Using pea-sized amounts for each boot, first model a long teardrop and pinch up the full end. Hollow this out slightly, using the end of a paintbrush, then stick the boot onto the end of the leg using sugar glue. Use foam pieces for support.

## Grass and flowers

**13** To make the grass, roll the remaining green into different-sized sausages, tapering at one end. Indent down the centre using a cocktail stick (toothpick).

Stick in place in clusters, bending over the tips. For the flowers, thinly roll out yellow trimmings and cut out star shapes with the small cutter. Indent each petal with a cocktail stick and place the flower on a piece of foam. To indent the centre, press the end of the paintbrush down into it, pushing down into the foam sponge to shape the flower.

## Magical touches

**14** Sprinkle green pollen dust around the cake board and put a tiny amount of orange pollen dust into each flower. Brush a small amount of edible gold powder over the rocks.

**15** Add only a tiny touch of turquoise food colouring paste to the piping gel and stir well. Pour the coloured gel into the waterfall and spread out carefully, using the paintbrush. Put a few drips onto the sprites' hands and a few more drips around the cake and board.

d

e

# Sea Witch

Deep under the sea, what would a beautiful Sea Witch live in? I imagined a tall and jagged cave with a treasure of black pearls and a sea serpent to guard it.

## Cake & decoration

(See pages 7–13 for recipes and cake chart)

10cm (4in), 12cm (5in), 18cm (7in) round cakes

30cm (12in) round cake board

1.25kg (2½lb) sugarpaste (rolled fondant)

Jade green, cream, dark green, black, blue and pink food colouring pastes

Icing (powdered) sugar in a shaker

470g (15oz/scant 2 cups) buttercream

Sugar glue

375g (12oz) modelling paste

Dark green powder food colouring

Edible pale blue sparkle powder

Edible green glitter

## Equipment

Large rolling pin

Plain and serrated kitchen knives

Small glue brush

Fine and medium paintbrushes

Pieces of foam sponge

Templates (see page 94)

A few cocktail sticks

No. 4 plain piping tube (tip)

Dusting brush

## Cake board and cake

1 Colour 375g (12oz) of sugarpaste (rolled fondant) pale jade. Roll out and cover the cake board, marking ridges with the rolling pin. Trim the crust from the cakes and slice flat. Put one on top of the other, graduating in size. Leaving a 2.5cm (1in) circle centrally on the top, cut down at an angle, taking off the top edge of each cake, creating the sloping sides and leaving a ridge around the top of the base cake. Cut out a wedge of cake for the cave opening. Cut a layer in each cake and sandwich back together with buttercream. Colour 875g (1¾lb) of sugarpaste jade. Model 15g (½oz) into a teardrop and use to heighten the cake, smoothing the sides level with the cake surface. Roll 60g (2oz) into a tapering sausage, then place the fullest part *(see a)* on the ridge at the back of the cake and bring the two points around to the front. Smooth the sides level with the ridge. Position

a

the cake centrally on the board. Spread buttercream over the surface of the cake.

2 Roll out the remaining jade sugarpaste and sprinkle with icing sugar to prevent sticking. Roll up, place against the cake and unroll around it, pushing gently into the cave opening. Pinch the top into a point. Trim excess at the join, stick together with sugar glue, then rub gently with your fingertips to remove. Trim excess from around the base. Pinch sharp edges around the cave opening and along the ridges to make them angular. Indent more ridges around the cake and mark lines by rolling with the paintbrush handle (see b).

## Sea witch

3 Colour 60g (2oz) of modelling paste deep jade. Put aside 7g (¼oz). To make the dress, roll the remainder into a sausage, tapering to a point at one end. Pinch around the full end to shape the waist and round off the chest area,

then cut the top straight (see c). Stick in place and hold until secure.

4 Colour 125g (4oz) of modelling paste jade. To make the cauldron, split 60g (2oz) in half and roll into a ball. Press in the centre to indent and pinch around the edge to create the dish. Using the remaining half, split into three pieces, graduating in size, and model them into angular rocks. Assemble the pieces, sticking with sugar glue.

5 Colour just over 7g (¼oz) of modelling paste cream. Put aside two pea-sized amounts and, from the remainder, model the chest and neck area, and separate head and nose. First, shape a sausage with a neck pinched out from the top. Cut the bottom straight and stick in position. For her head, roll into an oval shape and narrow the chin area by stroking downwards either side. Stick in place against the cake, then model her tiny ball nose.

6 Put aside a pea-sized amount of deep jade modelling paste, then split the remainder in half. To make a sleeve, roll a sausage, rounding off one end, and pinch to open up. Twist and roll down the end of the sleeve to a point. Bend the sleeve half way by indenting at the front and pinching out at the back. Make the second sleeve in the same way and stick both in place (see d).

7 Stick on two minute flattened circles of white for eyes and two smaller deep jade circles for the iris. Use the pea-sized amounts of cream to make the hands. Shape one into a teardrop shape. From the pointed end, cut a thumb on one side, then three further cuts at the top to separate fingers. Twist each finger until long and pointed. Pinch gently at the rounded end to make a wrist and stick into a sleeve. If necessary, use a piece of foam sponge for support until dry. Make the second hand, cutting an opposite thumb.

b

c

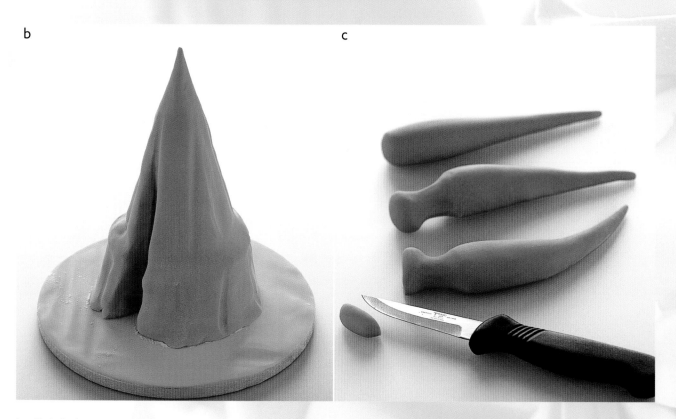

**8** Colour 90g (3oz) of modelling paste pale jade. Using the templates, roll out and cut the tail fins and the four dress veils, marking into each by rolling over the surface with the paintbrush handle. Stick the veils in place, with the largest one curling up towards the top of the cave. Colour 7g (¼oz) of paste dark green for seaweed. Roll into thin sausages of different lengths and press flat. Indent down each side and stroke outwards to round each leaf (see e). Stick in position, following the direction of the dress veils.

**9** For hair, colour 45g (1½oz) of modelling paste black. Shape half into a teardrop and stick onto her head as a frame for her hair, smoothing the point against the cave. Roll the remainder into thin tapering sausage shapes of different lengths. Stick over the frame, twisting them up and securing against the cave. Model some shorter pieces and curl them around her face. Model two tiny pupils for her eyes and roll 10–15 tiny pearls.

### Rocks and sea serpent

**10** Using the remaining jade modelling paste, model different-sized spiked rocks by pinching and twisting each upwards, a twisted wand and all the rocks of varying sizes. Stick the wand in the witch's hand and all the rocks around the base of the cake. Colour 15g (½oz) of modelling paste dusky blue, using blue with a touch of black. Reserve a tiny piece. To make the sea serpent, roll the paste into a tapering sausage and press the full end to flatten the eye area. Cut the mouth open with the knife. With the remaining deep jade, roll two tiny eyes. To make the fin, press a tapering sausage flat and mark lines radiating from the centre using the knife.

### Shells and fish

**11** For shells, knead 7g (¼oz) of white with a little jade until marbled. Shape into teardrops and press in the centre. Turn over and mark radiating lines with a cocktail stick (toothpick). Colour the remaining paste pale dusky blue and make three fish by modelling small sausages and pinching a head at the end. Pinch the opposite end to a point, make a low cut and reshape for the tail fins. Model separate fins, marking each with a cocktail stick; use the tip to indent eyes. Mark the smile by indenting with the piping tube (tip). Stick on tiny dusky blue stripes.

### Magical touches

**12** To create shadow, brush dark green powder into the doorway. Brush the cake base and board with sparkle powder. Using sugar glue, paint over the serpent's eyes and the patches, lines over the seaweed and hair, then sprinkle with green glitter. Put glitter into the cauldron. Dilute black food colouring with water and paint the eyeliner and eyebrows. Dilute pink food colouring and paint her lips.

d

e

# Flying Fun

Witches have to learn their craft somewhere. In this school for witches, little apprentices are happily whizzing around the towers, learning to fly broomsticks properly.

## Cake & decoration

(See pages 7–13 for recipes and cake chart)
2 x 15cm (6in) round cakes and
1 x 18cm (7in) round cake
25cm (10in) round cake board
125g (4oz) modelling paste
Brown, green, black, purple, blue, turquoise, yellow, cream and golden brown food colouring pastes
Icing (powdered) sugar in a shaker
45g (1½oz) royal icing
Sugar glue
Edible silver glitter
1.345kg (2lb 11oz) sugarpaste (rolled fondant)
440g (14oz/1¾ cups) buttercream
3 sugar sticks

## Equipment

Fine paintbrush
Large and small rolling pins
Plain and serrated kitchen knives
Foam sheet
Templates (see page 93)
No.1 plain piping tube (tip)
Miniature, 8cm (3in) and 8.5cm (3¼in) circle cutters
1.5cm (¾in) and 2.5cm (1in) square cutters
4 paper piping bags
Pieces of foam sponge

## Witches' brooms and door

**1** Make the witches' brooms first to allow plenty of drying time (see a). Colour 45g (1½oz) of modelling paste brown. Split 7g (¼oz) into six pieces, with one slightly smaller, and roll the sausage-shaped broomsticks. Mark the surface, using the paintbrush to indent a wood effect. Roll out 7g (¼oz), cut into little strips for twigs and stick around the bottom of five broomsticks only. Cut strips and wrap around the top of the twigs, crossing over at the front. Colour a quarter of the royal icing light brown and pipe more twigs on each. Brush each broomstick with sugar glue and sprinkle with edible glitter. Place each broomstick on the foam sheet to dry. Roll out the remaining brown and cut out the door, using the template. Mark wood lines with a knife and scratch wood grain with a cocktail stick (toothpick). Using trimmings, make the door handle and then roll out and cut two strips for

a

the door. Stick in place and indent along each strip using the No.1 plain piping tube (tip). Place on the foam sheet to dry.

## Flying school

**2** Colour 315g (10oz) of sugarpaste (rolled fondant) green, roll out and cover the cake board completely, trimming excess from around the edge. Trim the crust from each cake and level the top of each. Cut layers and sandwich the two smaller cakes together, making the base of the school, and position on the cake board. From the larger cake, cut two 8cm (3in) circles and sandwich together for the tower, and an 8.5cm (3¼in) circle for the roof. Trim the top edge of this roof cake to shape the sloping sides (see b). Spread all cakes with a layer of buttercream to help the sugarpaste stick, including the roof underside.

**3** Colour 15g (½oz) of sugarpaste dark grey. Thinly roll out and cut the doorway and

window, using the templates (see page 93). Stick in place, smoothing the surface with a cake smoother. Colour the remaining sugarpaste pale grey. Using 410g (13oz), roll out a little at a time and cut squares using the square cutters. Cut more squares and oblong shapes from these, making bricks, and build up around the base of the school (see c).

**4** Roll out 100g (3½oz) of pale grey sugarpaste and cut a circle to cover the top of the base cake. Place the tower cake centrally on top and cover with bricks as before. Roll out 45g (1½oz) of pale grey, place the base of the roof down onto it and cut around. Roll out 100g (3½oz) and cover the top, trimming away excess and smoothing into a point (see d). Stick onto the top of the tower with sugar glue.

**5** Knead a touch of purple food colouring paste into 30g (1oz) of pale grey sugarpaste. Roll out

and cut a strip the width of the doorway for the path and stick in place, smoothing down each side and trimming excess from the edge of the cake board. Cut out squares for the top edge of the base cake using 75g (2½oz) of pale grey. With the remaining pale grey, cut out a square, using the larger square cutter, and cut into three strips. Bend each in the centre and use to edge around the underside of the roof. Cut another strip to fit the length of the window ledge. Model three flattened circles to edge the top of the window and doorway, then make the doorbell and roof finial.

## Apprentice witches

**6** To make the witches, first colour just over 7g (¼oz) of modelling paste blue, then 7g (¼oz) each of turquoise, purple, yellow and cream, and the remaining piece black. Each figure is built up on a broomstick and allowed to dry before positioning, except for the girl flying out of the

b

c

tower window, so stick the smaller broomstick into the window, supported by the window ledge.

**7** To make trousers, roll 7g (¼oz) of modelling paste into a fat sausage and press to flatten slightly. Make a cut three-quarters of the way down to separate legs (see e for modelled shapes). Smooth to remove the ridges on both sides and pinch half way to bend the knees. Press at the bottom of each leg to flatten and then stick onto the centre of a broomstick. For shoes, roll pea-sized amounts into oval shapes and stick onto each trouser, pinching gently in the centre to arch the foot.

**8** To make a top, split just under 7g (¼oz) of modelling paste in half and, with one half, model a teardrop shape. Indent at the full end to hollow slightly, and stick onto the trousers. Split the remaining piece in half and use to make two sleeves, bending half way and pinching gently to shape the

elbow. Hollow out the end of each sleeve, using the end of the paintbrush, so the hands will slot in easily, and stick in place. Use pea-sized amounts of cream for each hand. Model into teardrop shapes and flatten slightly. Cut a thumb to one side and three cuts along the top of the rounded end to separate fingers. Pinch each finger gently to lengthen and twist at the wrist, bringing up a little point that will slot into the end of each sleeve, and secure with sugar glue.

**9** Push a sugar stick down through the top of each figure, leaving half protruding to help hold the head in place. Split the remaining cream into three and model teardrop-shaped heads with tiny ball noses. Make a hole into the base of each using a cocktail stick, then press down onto the sugar stick, securing at the base with sugar glue. Indent smiles using the miniature circle cutter pressed in at an angle, then dimple the corners using the cocktail stick.

**10** Split 7g (¼oz) of black modelling paste into three pieces. Model the three hats from teardrop shapes, hollowing out the full end and pinching a rim, and then twist up a long point. Thinly roll out the remainder and cut the cloaks and collars using the template (see page 93). To mark pleats in each cloak, gently roll over the surface with the paintbrush handle.

**11** Split the royal icing into three and colour dark brown, light brown and golden brown. Stick the remaining two figures and broomsticks against the school, using royal icing, and hold for a few moments until secure. Using the piping bags, with a small hole cut into the tip, pipe the hair, flicking up at the ends. When the cake is dry, dilute black colouring paste with a little water and paint their eyes using the fine paintbrush. Randomly paint a little sugar glue over the cake and figures, and sprinkle with a little edible glitter.

d

e

# Fairy Godmother

A book filled with magical cakes wouldn't be complete without a friendly Fairy Godmother waving her wand, sprinkling magic star dust everywhere and granting birthday wishes.

## Cake & decoration

(See pages 7–13 for recipes and cake chart)

2 litre (4 pint/10 cup) bowl-shaped cake

35cm (14in) round cake board

1kg (2lb) sugarpaste (rolled fondant)

Pink, blue, cream and black food colouring pastes

Icing (powdered) sugar in a shaker

315g (10oz) modelling paste

Sugar glue

410g (13oz/1⅔ cups) buttercream

8–10cm (3–4in) sugar stick or food safe dowelling

30g (1oz) royal icing

Edible pink sparkle powder

Edible silver glitter

## Equipment

Large rolling pin

Plain and serrated kitchen knives

Small glue brush

Paintbrush

Templates (see page 93)

A few cocktail sticks

Nos. 1, 4 and 17 plain piping tubes (tips)

Piping bag

Dusting brush

Pieces of foam sponge

## Cake board and wand

1 Colour 250g (8oz) of sugarpaste (rolled fondant) pink and 750g (1½lb) blue. Knead the pink and 250g (8oz) of blue together until streaky. Roll out and cover the cake board completely, trimming excess from around the edge, then put aside to dry.

2 To allow drying time for the wand, roll just under 7g (¼oz) of white modelling paste into a sausage, then put aside to dry.

## Fairy godmother's head

3 Make her head first to allow it time to set (see a). Colour 75g (2½oz) of modelling paste flesh, using cr… food colouring paste with a touch of pink. Put aside 7g (¼oz), roll the remainder into a ball and pinch out a rounded nose. Cut a curved line for her smile underneath, and smooth along the line with the damp

a

glue brush to open it up. Put a little more pressure at the centre of the bottom lip to pull it down slightly. Smooth along the bottom lip to round it off. Dimple each corner, using the end of the paintbrush. Roll two large pea-sized amounts and press onto her cheeks. Moisten either side of her nose with sugar glue, then blend the cheeks into her face to smooth and remove the joins completely.

## Cake

4 Trim the crust from the cake and slice the top flat, keeping a rounded edge. Cut a layer in the cake and sandwich back together with buttercream. Trim around the shape to create the pleats and folds. Use trimmings to make them deeper, sticking them in place with buttercream *(see b)*. Spread a layer over the surface of the cake to help the sugarpaste stick.

5 Roll out the remaining blue sugarpaste and cover the cake completely, smoothing around the shape and tucking any excess sugarpaste underneath. Position the cake on the cake board. Gently pinch the pleats for the gown to define them.

## Gown and cloak

6 Colour 75g (2½oz) of modelling paste blue. For her bodice, roll 45g (1½oz) into an oval shape, then roll in the centre to indent. Stick on top of the cake towards the front, so the skirt is fuller at the back *(see c)*. Split 30g (1oz) in half and use for sleeves. First, roll into a sausage, fuller at one end. Pinch into the full end to open up the sleeve and smooth around the edge to round off. Mark the elbow by bending half way, then pinch out at the back. Stick each sleeve in place level with the top of the bodice, bringing them together at the front with one sleeve slightly higher than the other. Secure against the gown.

7 To make the cloak, first colour 140g (4½oz) of modelling paste mauve, using pink and blue food colouring pastes. Roll out 75g (2½oz) and cut the cloak, using the template (see page 93). Moisten around her shoulders with sugar glue, then stick the cloak in position, pulling it around until joined at the neck. There will be a little excess around the top: just smooth it down, then press a little dip into it so that it will cradle the head. Push a sugar stick down into the body, leaving half protruding. Push the head down onto the sugar stick, securing with sugar glue at the base and tilt slightly.

8 Shape 30g (1oz) of mauve modelling paste into a teardrop shape and press into the full end, pinching up a rim. Stick in place on top of her head as a support for the hood. Roll out the remaining mauve and cut out the oblong-shaped hood, using the template (see page 93). Lay it against the front of the support *(see d)* and smooth the two far corners down, joining at the back

b

c

and tucking the two front corners under her chin. Glue the join at the back, then rub in a circular motion with the palm of your hand to remove completely.

**9** Thinly roll out the mauve trimmings and cut the bow, using the template (see page 93). Mark the surface to create pleats, fold each over and stick together under her chin. Finish the bow with a little square tie.

### Glasses and eyes

**10** Colour 7g (¼oz) of modelling paste pale grey, using a touch of black food colouring paste. To make the glasses, roll out a pea-sized amount and cut out three circles using the No. 17 plain piping tube (tip). From the centre of each, cut out another circle, using the No. 4 plain piping tube. Cut a little piece from one circle, making a bridge for the glasses, and assemble the glasses using sugar glue, and then set aside to dry. Split the remaining

grey in half and make her hair, tucking the ends around her face. Mark lines on the surface using the handle of the paintbrush.

**11** Stick on two tiny flattened oval-shaped eyes using white modelling paste, with two smaller oval-shaped iris using blue trimmings. Colour a minute amount of modelling paste black and make two pupils. Roll a tiny amount into two very thin sausages and use for eyelashes. Stick the glasses onto the end of her nose.

### Hands

**12** Split the remaining flesh-coloured modelling paste in half and use to make the hands, using the step photograph as a modelling guide (see e). Model two pea-sized amounts into teardrops and press slightly flat. Make a cut on one side for the thumb, then three cuts along the top to separate fingers. Pinch each finger to remove ridges and then pinch around the wrist to lengthen and

create an anchor that will slot easily into the end of each sleeve. Stick the hands to the wand, turning out each wrist, and then stick each wrist into the end of each sleeve. Secure the end of the wand to the dress.

### Magical touches

**13** Pipe small lines in a circle for the sparkles over her dress and the cake board, using royal icing and the piping bag fitted with the No. 1 plain piping tube. When dry, dust her cheeks and some of the sparkles with pink sparkle powder. Finally, dust a little edible silver glitter over the sparkles on the cake board.

d

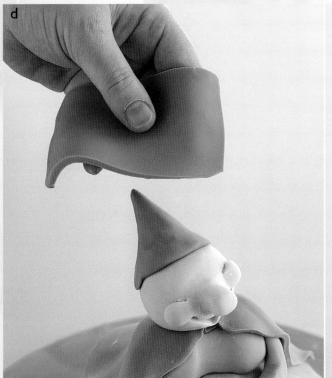

e

# Gold Mine

Little dwarfs, working busily in their gold mine, make an enchanting cake for any child. The pools of candlelight radiating from lamps, and sparkling nuggets of gold, complete the magic.

## Cake & decoration

(See pages 7–13 for recipes and cake chart)
20cm (8in) square cake
30cm (12in) round cake board
500g (1lb) modelling paste
Brown, black, cream, red and mauve food colouring pastes
Icing (powdered) sugar in a shaker
Sugar glue
410g (13oz/1⅔ cups) buttercream
1.22kg (2lb 7oz) sugarpaste (rolled fondant)
Edible gold powder
Yellow powder food colouring

## Equipment

Large rolling pin
1.5cm (¾in) square cutter
Plain and serrated kitchen knives
Small glue brush
A few cocktail sticks
Ruler
Medium paintbrush
Dusting brush
No. 4 plain piping tube (tip)
Pieces of foam sponge

## Pickaxes and ladder

1 To allow drying time, make three pickaxes and the ladder first. Colour 170g (5½oz) of modelling paste brown and 60g (2oz) grey. For the ladder, roll out 30g (1oz) of brown and cut out four squares in a line, with a step between each, using the square cutter. Cut around, creating a ladder with three steps. Mark the surface with a cocktail stick (toothpick) for a wood effect. For a pickaxe handle, roll a pea-sized amount of brown into a sausage and mark the surface as before. For the axe, roll a pea-sized amount of grey into a tapering sausage and stick to the handle. Bend the tip down. Make two more, then a brown ball for the tops.

## Cake and cake board

2 Trim the cake crust and slice the top flat. Cut as the cutting diagram (see page 95 and below). Trim the large and small rock cakes to round off, cut a layer

a

in each and sandwich back together with buttercream. Place the large rock cake towards the back of the cake board and sandwich the smaller rock on top. Trim at either end of the two carriage cakes, so they slope inwards towards the base. Arrange trimmings to create some steps around the large rock and pile a little at the front of the board. Spread the cakes with buttercream.

3 Colour 1kg (2lb) of sugarpaste (rolled fondant) grey using black food colouring paste. Roll out and cover the cake and cake board completely, smoothing around the shape and trimming excess from around the edge. Pinch around all rocks to make them angular and, using your fingers, stroke lines in the direction of the track. Model different-sized rocks with trimmings and pile up around the board, putting one on top of the small rock cake. Using 75g (2½oz) of brown paste to make the track, thinly roll out and cut strips

measuring 8cm (3in). Mark the surface of each by scratching wood lines using a cocktail stick, then stick in place. Roll out and cut two long strips for either side, stick in place and trim any excess (see b).

## Carriages and bucket

4 Colour 45g (1½oz) of sugarpaste black. Thinly roll out and place the top of a carriage down onto it and cut around. Cover the base and then cover the second carriage in the same way. Colour the remaining sugarpaste brown. To cover the carriage sides (see c), roll out a little at a time and indent evenly spaced lines by pressing in with a ruler. Scratch wood lines with a cocktail stick. Measure and cut out pieces to fit the sides, keeping them slightly higher than the cake. Cover the two longest sides first, then the ends. Stick both carriages onto the board, securing with sugar glue.

5 To make the bucket, roll 7g (¼oz) of brown modelling

paste into a ball and indent into the top to open. Press both ends down onto the work surface to flatten and roll the sides straight. Mark lines for wood, then stick onto the carriage. Roll out and cut a tiny strip for the handle, loop around and stick in position. For the wheels, split 15g (½oz) of brown modelling paste into eight pieces and shape into flattened circles. Stick in place with a tiny ball on the centre of each.

## Gnomes

6 To make the gnomes (see d), colour 45g (1½oz) of modelling paste dark cream, 60g (2oz) cream, 45g (1½oz) pale cream, 7g (¼oz) red, 15g (½oz) pale mauve and 22g (¾oz) orange, using red colouring with a little cream. Make one gnome at a time and build up each on the cake.

7 Use 7g (¼oz) of brown modelling paste, split in half, to make boots. To model, roll into a sausage and bend up one end,

b

c

pinching up a rim and hollowing it out slightly. Mark the pleats by pressing in and rolling a cocktail stick over the surface. The trousers are modelled from a 7g (¼oz) slightly flattened square. Cut down the centre to separate legs and smooth the ridges to remove. Mark pleats as before. Stick these directly onto the boots.

**8** Each top is made from just under 15g (½oz) of pale cream. Split in half and shape into a slightly flattened circle. Press one side down on the work surface to flatten the bottom. Split the remaining half in half again for two sausage-shaped sleeves, marking pleats as before. Indent into the end of each sleeve to open up so the hands will slot in easily. Bend each arm half way, press in at the front and pinch out at the back for elbows. Thinly roll out 7g (¼oz) for the tunic, then cut an oblong measuring 8 x 4cm (3 x 1½in) and place over the top and shoulders. Squeeze the sides together and

wrap a thinly cut strip of brown paste around the waist, crossing over at the front for a belt.

**9** To make a head, roll just under 15g (½oz) of cream modelling paste into a ball and pinch out a nose. Stick on two tiny flattened circles of white modelling paste for eyes and two pupils, made from black sugarpaste. Shape two small pea-sized teardrops for cheeks and edge each eye with tiny tapering sausages. The hands are made from slightly larger pea-sized amounts. Model into a teardrop and press slightly flat. Make a cut on one side for the thumb, then two cuts along the top to separate fingers. Pinch each finger to remove ridges and then pinch around the wrist to lengthen and create an anchor that will slot easily into the end of each of the sleeves.

**10** For the hat, roll a tapering sausage using just under 15g (½oz) of paste. Pinch deeply into the full end to open up, so it

fits neatly on top of the head. Bend and stick the end of the hat against the tunic. Using white modelling paste, model different lengths of tapering sausage shapes for hair, eyebrows, beard and moustache.

## Magical touches

**11** With the remaining grey paste, model little handles for the end of the carriages and all the small nuggets. Stick nuggets around the cake in clusters, put some spilling out of the bucket, and fill the second carriage. Paint the surface of the nuggets with sugar glue and leave until tacky. Brush over edible gold powder.

**12** For lamps (see e), colour the remaining modelling paste bright yellow and roll into balls. Using brown paste, make the lantern cases, cutting a hole into the handle at the top, using the No. 4 tube. Mix yellow powder with icing sugar and brush the cake near the lanterns for candlelight. Brush gold powder over the cake.

d

e

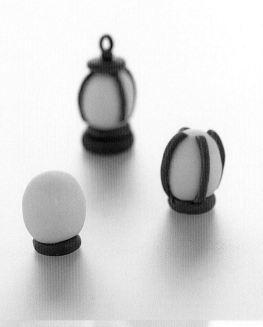

# Giant Troll

Children love stories about giants, and it doesn't matter whether they're scary or kind. I decided to make a friendly giant troll, about to squash everything in sight with his great boots.

## Cake & decoration

(See pages 7–13 for recipes and cake chart)

18cm (7in) and 20cm (8in) round cakes

30cm (12in) round cake board

2kg (4lb) sugarpaste (rolled fondant)

Flesh, mauve, cream, brown, black, golden brown and green food colouring pastes

500g (1lb/2 cups) buttercream

Icing (powdered) sugar in a shaker

Sugar glue

8cm (3in) sugar stick or length of food-safe dowelling

Mauve and green powder food colourings

## Equipment

Plain and serrated kitchen knives

Large sable paintbrush

Large rolling pin

Small glue brush

Pieces of foam sponge

Ball or bone tool

Templates (see page 94)

Small, pointed scissors

## Troll's head

**1** Make the head first to give time to set before being positioned. Colour 235g (7½oz) of sugarpaste (rolled fondant) flesh and roll 140g (4½oz) into a ball-shaped head. For the smile, press in the tip of a knife on either side, then stroke along the bottom edge to create the bottom lip. Push the end of a paintbrush into the mouth corners and push up slightly (see a). For the chin area, press in on both sides, using your thumbs. Push the paintbrush into the base of the head to make a hole for when the head is positioned later. If the back has flattened, reshape by gently rolling.

## Cake and cake board

**2** Trim the crust from each cake and slice the tops flat. Put the smaller cake centrally on top of the larger cake. Leaving a 5cm (2in) circle centrally on the top, cut down at an angle to the base to create the

a

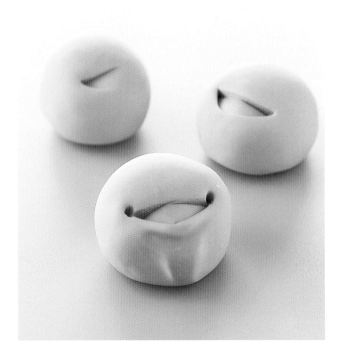

sloping sides of the mountain shape. For the rounded top, place a large piece of cake trimming on top of the cake and trim again.

**3** Position the shaped cake on the cake board. Sandwich all the layers together with buttercream. Spread the surface of the cake with buttercream to help the sugarpaste stick. Cut some more cake trimmings into strips and position these strips around the base of the cake (see b), then spread with buttercream.

**4** Colour 875g (1¾lb) of sugarpaste pale mauve. Roll out and cover the cake and cake board, smoothing into the ridges around the cake, and then trim excess from around the board edge. To make the snow, model several teardrops in different lengths, using 125g (4oz) of white sugarpaste. Stick around the top of the mountain, smoothing the joins closed at the top to resemble a snow-capped mountain (see c).

## Troll's clothes

**5** Colour 265g (8½oz) of sugarpaste cream. Using 140g (4½oz), roll a teardrop shape for the troll's shirt and pinch into the full end to hollow out. Press deeply into the surface, using the paint-brush handle to mark pleats, and press to flatten the neck area. Stick in place with the neck area level with the top of the mountain. (See back view photograph on page 86.) Split 60g (2oz) in half and roll sausage-shaped sleeves, marking pleats as before using the paintbrush handle. Bend the sleeves at the elbow and then secure with sugar glue.

**6** Colour 220g (7oz) of sugarpaste mid brown. Roll 200g (6½oz) into a fat sausage. Cut down the centre to separate legs and pinch around the bottom of each to widen and hollow out. Mark deep pleats as before, then stick against the mountain in a wide-legged pose. Smooth gently to round off and shape his bottom.

**7** With the remaining mid brown, thinly roll out and cut a trouser patch, then roll out and cut two slightly thicker strips for braces. Stick the braces over the shoulders, tucking into all the pleats, and cross over at the back. Stick the patch onto the trousers and mark different-sized stitches around the edge using a knife. Shape a flattened circle for a collar, using 15g (½oz) of cream, then cut out a 'v' from the edge to the circle centre.

## Troll's face

**8** Push the sugar stick or dowelling into the top of the mountain, leaving half protruding. Push the head down onto the sugar stick and secure at the base with sugar glue. Using 15g (½oz) of flesh, model two flattened circles for cheeks, shape his nose and make his toe, marking the toenail with a knife, then put aside. Split just under 7g (¼oz) of flesh in half and make two ears, indenting in the centre of each

b

c

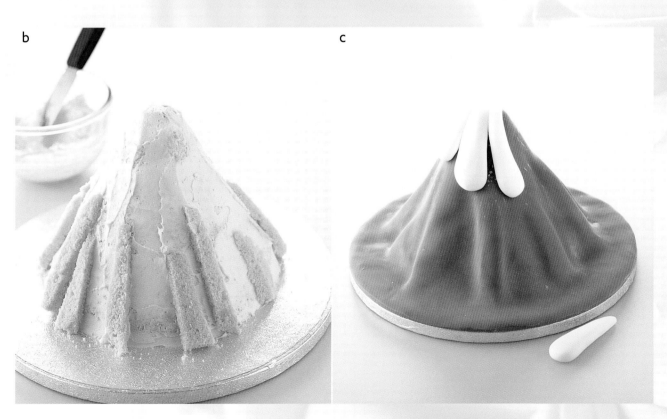

with your finger. Stick the two ears in place either side of his head, level with his nose.

**9** With pea-sized amounts of white for each eye, make two flattened oval-shaped eyes, then roll out and cut a small tooth. For the iris, model two flattened oval shapes using mid brown trimmings. Colour a pea-sized amount of black sugarpaste and model two pupils, and two tiny sausage-shaped eyebrows.

## Boots, hands and hair

**10** To make the troll's boots, first colour 185g (6oz) of sugarpaste pale brown. Split in half and shape into ovals. Pinch to narrow the heel and round off the toe area. Mark pleats in the boots using the paintbrush handle (see d). Cut a line at the front to mark the sole on one boot only, and then push into the toe area to open up. Stick the troll's boots in place, then position the toe made earlier. Use foam pieces for

support until the boots are completely dry.

**11** Split the remaining flesh in half to make the hands. Shape one piece into a teardrop shape and press to flatten slightly. Cut on one side for the thumb and cut twice into the top to separate fingers. Smooth to remove ridges and press down at the fingertips to widen. Stick in place, and then make the second hand, cutting the opposite thumb. Mark nails using a knife. Split the remaining cream sugarpaste in half and model the two cuffs, marking pleats with the paintbrush handle. Stick in place, hiding the join between the sleeves and hands.

**12** Colour 75g (2½oz) of sugarpaste golden brown. Using the templates (see page 94), roll out and cut the hair pieces, one at a time, starting with the largest piece first. Stick these in place on top of the troll's head and flick up some of the points.

Finish the hair by sticking on a small pointed trimming and smooth the join closed.

## Trees

**13** Colour the remaining sugarpaste green and split into several different-sized pieces. To make a tree (see e), model into a teardrop shape and then snip into the tree at an angle using scissors. Start at the top and make small cuts, gradually cutting in deeper as you spiral down, and then cut away the excess paste at the base. Bend one of the trees at the tip.

## Magical touches

**14** Mix mauve and green powder colourings separately with a little icing (powdered) sugar and then dust mauve into the ridge recesses around the mountain and dust green around the base, using the large paintbrush. Stick the trees in place, positioning the bent tree directly under the troll's boot.

d

e

# Crystal Ball

Here is a wizard with his giant crystal ball, large enough to play around with all the stars in the universe and turn the whole world in a spin.

## Cake & decoration

(See pages 7–13 for recipes and cake chart)

2 x 1 litre (2 pint/5 cup) bowl-shaped cakes

30cm (12in) round cake board

1.25kg (2½lb) sugarpaste (rolled fondant)

Blue, purple and cream food colouring pastes

Icing (powdered) sugar in a shaker

315g (10oz) modelling paste

Sugar glue

280g (9oz/1 generous cup) buttercream

Sugar stick

Edible silver glitter

## Equipment

Large rolling pin

Serrated and small/medium plain kitchen knives

Various star cutters

Small glue brush

Cake smoother

Template (see page 93)

Paintbrush

Pieces of foam sponge

A few cocktail sticks

Dusting brush

**1** Colour 750g (1½lb) of sugarpaste (rolled fondant) pale blue and 500g (1lb) purple. Knead together 200g (6½oz) of pale blue and 170g (5½oz) of purple until streaky and colours are just starting to blend. Roll out and cover the cake board, trimming excess, then put aside to dry. Trim the crust from both cakes and level the tops. Put the cakes together and check they make a ball shape. Sandwich the two cakes together. Spread the surface with buttercream and leave to set.

### Stars and crystal ball

**2** Colour 45g (1½oz) of modelling paste lilac using blue colouring paste with a touch of purple. Save just over 7g (¼oz) for the hat and belt, then roll out the remainder and cut the different-sized stars (see a). Stick a group together for the wizard's hand. Leave to dry. Add a little more buttercream to the cake. Knead the remaining sugarpaste until streaky as before, roll out and cover the cake. Pull up a pleat and cut away

a

excess, without cutting away too much (see b). Pinch the join together and rub with icing sugar to remove. Smooth around the shape and trim. Position on the board.

## Wizard

**3** Colour 220g (7oz) of modelling paste deep mauve using blue and purple food colouring pastes. To make the wizard, model a long teardrop-shaped body 12cm (5in) in height, using 140g (4½oz), and press down on the full end to flatten. Thinly roll out 60g (2oz) of deep mauve and cut the cloak using the template (see page 93). Roll the paintbrush handle over the surface to create pleats. Stick in place, pulling out at the back for fullness and letting excess drape onto the cake board. For the staff, roll the trimmings into a sausage, tapering to a point. Flatten the top and pinch the surface to indent.

**4** Reserve a tiny amount for eyes, then split the remaining deep mauve paste in half for the sleeves. Model long teardrop shapes first, then pinch into the full end to open up. Twist down the end of each sleeve to a tapering point. Bend the arm half way and pinch out an elbow. Stick in position with the shoulders, level with the top of the body, one arm against the cloak and the other resting against the cake. Stick the staff in place using foam for support (see c). Push the sugar stick down through the top of his body, leaving a little protruding.

**5** Colour 7g (¼oz) of modelling paste cream and put aside two pea-sized amounts. Using the remainder, model an oval-shaped nose and roll a ball-shaped head. Mark the smile using the end of a paintbrush. Push the head down onto the sugar stick and secure at the base. Stick on his nose. For the rope belt, roll a thin sausage, using a little lilac modelling paste. Indent along the length at an angle, using the side of a cocktail stick. Cut into three strips and assemble his belt. For his hat, roll the remaining lilac paste into a teardrop with a long point. Indent at the full end to hollow and pinch out a wide rim. Stick onto his head slightly towards the back and hold until secure.

**6** Using the remaining white paste, make his hair and beard. Stick two long pieces under his nose for a moustache. For hands, see page 77, step 8. Stick into the sleeve ends, with one hand holding stars and the other the staff. Model tiny oval eyes, using deep mauve paste, and stick on tiny white sausages for eyebrows, marking hairs by pressing along the length at an angle with a cocktail stick. Moisten a line, spiralling around the cake and board, with sugar glue. Stick on all the stars, some flat, with others upright, and sprinkle along the line with a tiny amount of glitter. Brush glue over his hat, staff, eyes, around the cloak edges, and randomly over the stars, then brush with glitter.

b                                    c

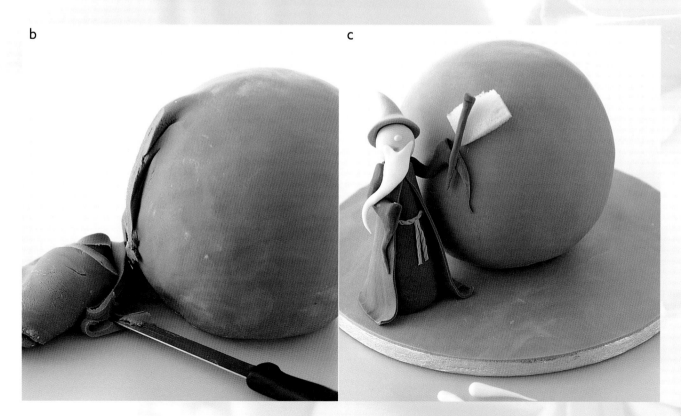

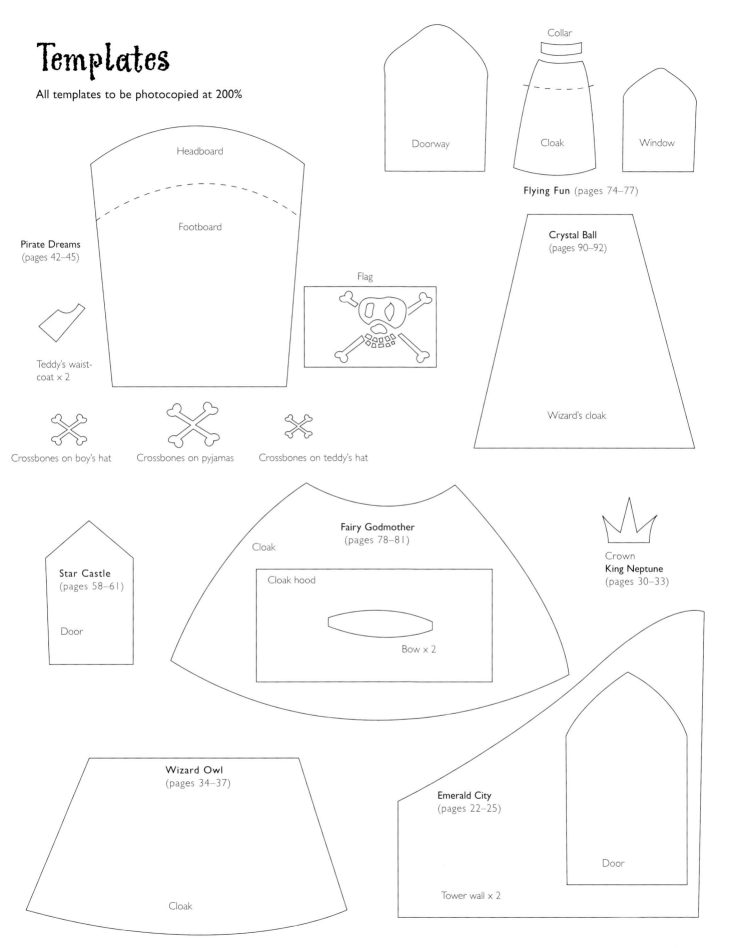

# Templates

All templates to be photocopied at 200%

Doorway

Collar

Cloak

Window

**Flying Fun** (pages 74–77)

Headboard

Footboard

**Pirate Dreams**
(pages 42–45)

Teddy's waist-
coat × 2

Flag

**Crystal Ball**
(pages 90–92)

Wizard's cloak

Crossbones on boy's hat

Crossbones on pyjamas

Crossbones on teddy's hat

**Star Castle**
(pages 58–61)

Door

Cloak

**Fairy Godmother**
(pages 78–81)

Cloak hood

Bow × 2

Crown
**King Neptune**
(pages 30–33)

**Wizard Owl**
(pages 34–37)

Cloak

**Emerald City**
(pages 22–25)

Door

Tower wall × 2

All templates to be photocopied at 200%

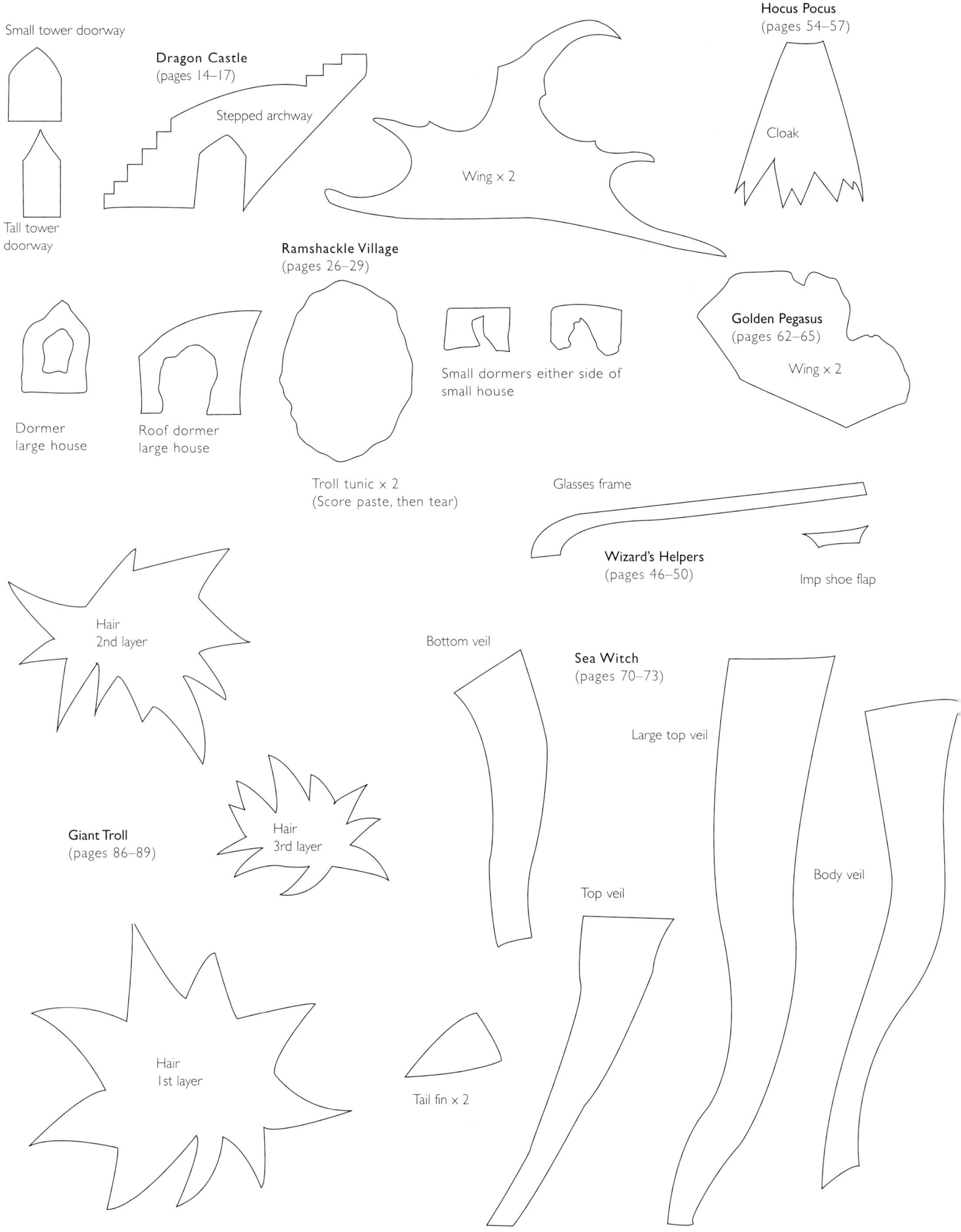

Small tower doorway

**Dragon Castle**
(pages 14–17)

Stepped archway

Wing x 2

**Hocus Pocus**
(pages 54–57)

Cloak

Tall tower
doorway

**Ramshackle Village**
(pages 26–29)

Dormer
large house

Roof dormer
large house

Small dormers either side of
small house

**Golden Pegasus**
(pages 62–65)

Wing x 2

Troll tunic x 2
(Score paste, then tear)

Glasses frame

**Wizard's Helpers**
(pages 46–50)

Imp shoe flap

Hair
2nd layer

Bottom veil

**Sea Witch**
(pages 70–73)

Large top veil

**Giant Troll**
(pages 86–89)

Hair
3rd layer

Top veil

Body veil

Hair
1st layer

Tail fin x 2

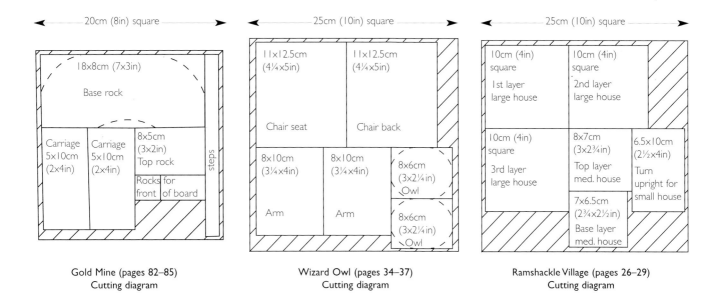

Gold Mine (pages 82–85)
Cutting diagram

Wizard Owl (pages 34–37)
Cutting diagram

Ramshackle Village (pages 26–29)
Cutting diagram

# Suppliers

The author and publisher would like to thank the following suppliers:

## UK suppliers
Culpitt Cake Art
Jubilee Industrial Estate
Ashington
Nthumb. NE63 8UQ
Tel: +44 (0)1670 814 545

Guy, Paul & Co Ltd
Unit B4, Foundry Way
Little End Road
Eaton Socon
Cambs PE19 3JH
Tel: +44 (0)1480 472 545

Renshaw Scott Ltd
Crown Street
Liverpool L8 7RF
Tel: +44 (0)151 706 8200
(Manufacturer of Regalice sugarpaste used in book)

Squires Kitchen
Squires House
3 Waverley Lane
Farnham, Surrey GU9 8BB
Tel: +44 (0)1252 711 749

## Other distributors and retailers
Corteil & Barratt
40 High Street
Ewell Village
Epsom, Surrey
KT17 1RW
Tel: +44 (0)20 8393 0032

Pipedreams
2 Bell Lane
Eton Wick, Berkshire
Tel: +44 (0)1753 865 682

Sugar Daddy's
No.1 Fishers Yard
Market Square, St Neots
Cambridgeshire
PE19 2AF
Tel: +44 (0)1480 471200

Confectionery Supplies
31 Lower Cathedral Road
Riverside, Cardiff
South Glamorgan, Wales
Tel: +44 (0)1222 372 161

Edable Art Ltd
1 Stanhope Close
The Grange, Spennymoor
County Durham DL16 6LZ
Tel/fax: +44 (0)1388 816309

Sugarflair Colours Ltd
Brunel Road
Manor Trading Estate
Benfleet
Essex SS7 4PS
Tel: +44 (0)1286 752 891

The British Sugarcraft Guild
Tel: +44 (0)20 8859 6943

National Sugar Art Assoc.
Tel: +44 (0)20 8777 4445

## Non-UK
Cakes & Co
25 Rock Hill
Blackrock Village
Co. Dublin
Ireland
Tel: +353 (0)1 283 6544

Beryl's Cake Decorating & Pastry Supplies
PO Box 1584
N. Springfield, USA
Tel: +1 800 488 2749

European Cake Gallery
844 North Crowley Road
Crowley, Texas 76036
USA
Tel: +1 817 297 2240

Creative Cutters
561 Edward Avenue,
Unit 1, Richmond Hill
Ontario, L4C 9W6
Canada
Tel: +1 905 883 5638

The Cake Decorators' School of Australia
Shop 7
Port Phillip Arcade
232 Flinders Street
Melbourne
Victoria 3000
Australia
Tel: +61 (0)3 9654 5335
Fax: +61 (0)3 9654 5818

Suzy Q Cake Decorating Centre
Shop 4
372 Keilor Road
Niddrie, Victoria 3042
Australia
Tel: +61 (0)3 9379 2275

Ediciones Ballina Codai S.A.
Avda Cordoba 2415
1st Floor, C1120Aag
Buenos Aires
Argentina
Tel: +5411 4962 5381
Fax: +5411 4963 3751

# Index

## a
almond madeira sponge cake, 7

## b
Baby Dragon, 12, 51–3
backpacks, 21
baking chart, 12–13
beds, 42-5
books, 48
boots, 89
bottles, 48-9
brooms, witches', 74
buckets, 84
buttercream, 8

## c
cake boards, covering, 11
cakes:
    covering, 11
    quantities, 12–13
    recipe, 7
    sculpting, 11
camp fire, 21
carriages, 84
castles:
    Dragon Castle, 14–17
    Labyrinth, 38–41
    Star Castle, 58–61
chair of wisdom, 34–6
cloaks, 37, 80–1
clouds, 60–1, 65
CMC (carboxy methyl cellulose), 8
colours, 9
    colouring sugarpaste, 11
Crystal Ball, 12, 90–2
cutting diagrams, 95

## d
dragons:
    Baby Dragon, 51–3
    Dragon Castle, 14–17

## e
edible glitter, 9
eggshells, 51–2
elfins, 20–1
Emerald City, 12, 22–5
equipment, 10

## f
fairies, 22–5
Fairy Godmother, 13, 78–81
fish, 73
flowers, 69
Flying Fun, 12, 74–7
food colouring paste, 9

## g
Giant Troll, 13, 86–9
glasses, 37, 81
glitter, edible, 9
glue, sugar, 9
gnomes, 41, 84–5
Gold Mine, 12, 82–5
Golden Pegasus, 12, 62–5
grass, 69
gum tragacanth, 8

## h
Hocus Pocus, 12, 54–7
horses, seafoam, 62–5

## i
icing, royal, 8
imps, 49–50

## k
King Neptune, 13, 30–3

## l
Labyrinth, 13, 38–41
ladder, 82

## m
madeira sponge cake, 7
modelling paste, 8

## n
Neptune, King, 30–3

## o
Owl, Wizard, 34–7

## p
Pegasus, Golden, 62–5
pickaxes, 82
Pirate Dreams, 12, 42–5
powder food colouring, 9
princess, 61

## r
Ramshackle Village, 13, 26–9
rocks:
    Rock Monster, 18–21

Sea Witch, 73
Sprite Waterfall, 66–9
rolled fondant see sugarpaste
royal icing, 8

## s
scrolls, 37
sculpting cakes, 11
seafoam horses, 32
sea serpent, 73
Sea Witch, 12, 70–3
shells, 30–1, 73
sponge cake, madeira, 7
Sprite Waterfall, 13, 66–9
Star Castle, 13, 58–61
stars, 65, 90–2
storing cakes, 9
sugar glue, 9
sugar sticks, 9
sugarpaste (rolled fondant):
    colouring, 11
    covering boards, 11
    covering cakes, 11
    marbling, 7
    preparation, 11
    recipe, 7
    sugar glue, 9

## t
techniques, 11
templates, 93–4
towers, 16, 38, 60–1
trees, 89
trident, 30
trolls:
    Giant Troll, 13, 86–9
    Ramshackle Village, 26–9

## w
Waterfall, Sprite, 66–9
wings, 17, 25, 37, 64, 69
witches:
    Flying Fun, 74–7
    Hocus Pocus, 54–7
    Sea Witch, 70–3
wizards:
    Crystal Ball, 90–2
    Wizard Owl, 13, 34–7
    Wizard's Helpers, 12, 46–50

First published in 2002 by Murdoch Books UK Ltd
Merehurst is an imprint of Murdoch Books UK Ltd
Reprinted 2002, 2004

Design and photography copyright © Murdoch Books UK Ltd 2002
Text and cake design copyright © Debra Brown 2002
Debra Brown has asserted her right under the Copyright, Designs and Patents Act, 1988.

ISBN 1-90399 233 8
A catalogue record for this book is available from the British Library.
All rights reserved. No part of this publication may be reproduced, stored in a retrieval system, or transmitted in any form or by any means, electronic, mechanical, photocopying, recording or otherwise, without the prior permission of the copyright owner.

Commissioning/Project Editor: Barbara Croxford
Designer: Shahid Mahmood
Design Manager: Sarah Rock
Photographer: Clive Streeter

CEO: Juliet Rogers
Publisher: Kay Scarlett

Colour separation by Colourscan, Singapore
Printed by Tien Wah Press, Malaysia

Murdoch Books UK Ltd
Erico House, 6th Floor North
93-99, Upper Richmond Road
Putney, London SW15 2TG
Tel: +44 (0)20 8785 5995
Fax: +44 (0)20 8785 5985
Murdoch Books UK Ltd is a subsidiary of Murdoch Magazines Pty Ltd.

Murdoch Books® Australia
Pier 8/9, 23 Hickson Road
Millers Point NSW 2000
Australia
Tel: +61 (0)2 4352 7000
Fax: +61 (0)2 4352 7026
Murdoch Books® is a trademark of Murdoch Magazines Pty Ltd